MUNICH 72

By the same author

The Red Snow (*With Sir John Hunt*)

Sportsmen of Our Time

Tokyo 1964—*A Diary of the XVIIIth Olympiad*

Mexico 1968—*A Diary of the XIXth Olympiad*

MUNICH 72

Christopher Brasher

STANLEY PAUL London

STANLEY PAUL & CO LTD
3 Fitzroy Square, London W1

AN IMPRINT OF THE HUTCHINSON GROUP

London Melbourne Sydney
Auckland Wellington Johannesburg Cape Town
and agencies throughout the world

★

First published 1972

This book has been set in Times and printed in Great Britain on Antique wove paper by The Camelot Press Ltd, London and Southampton

ISBN 0 09 114360 8

When I was an athlete, one journalist above all seemed to me to express the aspirations and feelings of an athlete. When I became a journalist I marvelled at his skill and professionalism. From the Berlin Games in 1936 to Munich in 1972, he has consistently illuminated the sporting scene. Now he has retired and we shall miss the depth of his knowledge and his gentlemanly presence. With admiration, therefore, this book is dedicated to

PETER WILSON

IN MEMORIAM

David Berger
Zeev Friedmann
Yosef Gottfreund
Eliezer Halfin
Yosef Romano
Amitzur Shapira
Kehat Shorr
Mark Slavin
Andre Spitzer
Yaacov Springer
Moshe Weinberg

ACKNOWLEDGEMENTS

The author acknowledges the following for their permission to reproduce illustrations of which they own the copyright:

Associated Press, Stewart Fraser (Colorsport)

E. D. Lacey, London Express, Syndication International

CONTENTS

ILLUSTRATIONS

Between pages 52 & 53

INTRODUCTION

'I experienced level after level of grief; for my own event, the marathon, for those years of preparation now useless; for the dead and doomed Israelis; and for the violated sanctuary of the Games.'

So wrote Kenny Moore, the American marathon runner, about the day that terror came to the Olympic Village. In that one sentence he has incorporated Olympic sport, Olympic and world violence, and the shattering of an ideal. I have in this book tried to do the same and I am only too aware that sometimes the contrast of emotions is almost insupportable.

But this is my record of what I experienced during those unbelievable three weeks. I do not pretend that it is complete or definitive, but I hope that the essentials are here, and if they are then I would like to thank my colleagues on *The Observer*, Peter Deeley and David Hunn, for the information which they have supplied about the day of the hostages. And I would also like to thank John Rodda of *The Guardian* and John Rafferty of *The Scotsman* for providing chapters on Rowing and Boxing—sports which I was not able to watch.

Lastly, the book would never have been completed without the help of Mrs. June Ormiston who put it all together through many long evenings.

October 1972

Christopher Brasher
Petersham
England

1
'WHERE THERE WAS NOISE THERE WAS DAVE'

'The only thing that matters in 1972 is those games in Munich—the pinnacle of my dreams, the result of every painful stride I have spent in training, the results of countless hours work, of running the equivalent of round the world, and more, on my two pins. I will run the Olympics from the front and grind the other runners into the track. . . .'—Dave Bedford in *The Dave Bedford Story*

For me the Dave Bedford story starts in a remote settlement in the mountains of Sweden—a place called Valadalen where an old and somewhat lonely man ran through the woods in the summer and skied along the tracks in the winter, right up to the time that he died in the summer of 1972 at the age of 77.

There is only one easy way to get to Valadalen and that is by helicopter and if you use it you destroy the quality of the place—the clean, still air and the unworldly peace. Otherwise you fly to Stockholm, and then northwards in an old piston-engined plane to Ostersund. Then you take the road to Trondheim, in Norway, and turn off to the left when the mountains start to get big—not big in the Alpine sense, but big like the Cairngorms. Indeed, the country is very similar—original forest, lakes and streams, with big hills rolling bare into the distance. Valadalen is a tiny village of wooden houses, two thousand feet up, resting on the lower slopes of a four-thousand-foot mountain, and looking across a forested plain to mountains in every direction. The main building is what the Scandinavians call a 'tourist station' and what we would call a mountain hotel. It is made of logs and it is unbelievably warm and comfortable and the food is good. Behind it there is a low log house with a roof covered in grass which gets so tall in summer that it needs to be scythed. It was in that low log house that the old man who ran and skied, Gosta Ollander, lived when Dave Bedford and I visited him in the summer of 1971. He was small and very brown and rather wizened but his face was still powerful.

My journey to Valadalen was peopled by ghosts—the ghosts of Sonja Henie, Herb Elliott, Ingemar Johannson, Michael Jazy, Sixten Jenberg (who was for cross-country skiing what Jean-Claude Killy was for downhill skiing) and many others. Above all, it was dominated by the ghost of Gundar Haegg. From the ancient log house amidst the trees and the hills and the breathless silence, Gundar Haegg descended during the war years, to do battle with Arne Andersson and clip, second by second, the world record for the English mile until it teetered on the brink of four minutes. Those races were the reading of my school days. So, to visit Valadalen and the old man who presided, Gosta Ollander, was, for me, a pilgrimage. For Dave Bedford, who spent ten days there in the summer of 1971 it was an escape from the pressure of expectations.

From the time he was 18 years old it was possible to rate Bedford as one of the truly great attractions of athletics. People wanted, and still want, to see him, and hear about him, as they wanted to see Zatopek or Kuts or Elliott, but there is a difference—Dave Bedford still has to prove himself against world class opposition. He could, and can, run magnificently, recording faster times than anyone in Britain (before Munich he held seven British records), faster times than anybody has ever run in the world except for Ron Clarke. But he held no international track titles. Dave went to Valadalen to prepare himself for the greatest race of his life, the 10,000 metres in the European championships, and to escape the pressure which had been building up around him.

Four weeks before the European championships, Dave ran the greatest solo 10,000 metres that it has ever been my privilege to watch. It was on a hot day, on a sandy track in Portsmouth, and he ran the distance in the second fastest time ever recorded in the world. And then, only two weeks later, he ran off the track in the middle of a race at the Crystal Palace. Success had turned into a ghastly nightmare. This is how his mother described it in a letter which she wrote to me the day after that traumatic happening at Crystal Palace: 'These last two weeks since the 10,000 metres race at Portsmouth have been of nightmare quality both for Dave and for us, his family. There had been so much publicity to fill the Crystal Palace stadium for the games and we seemed to have reporters and TV men here almost non-stop, with the phone ringing with barely a break in between. During this time Dave has been trying to train in his usual thorough way, but I know that towards the end of this last week there was so much tension in the home that the atmosphere was explosive. There will be many people better qualified than I who will hold a post-mortem about it: too much training; too much boasting; and all the rest. But I think it was simply that it was due to the almost unbelievable pressure of publicity. The rest of the family are all nervous wrecks and we didn't have to run the race!'

So the day after that race at the Crystal Palace, Dave went to Sweden, to Valadalen where you can run for miles through the forests and where the hills roll into the distance and where there seems to be nobody else in the world: that was where Dave had his hideout—with Gaston Roelants, the Belgian Olympic gold medallist, as his companion. Together, in the early morning, they ran for an hour, had a shower and then came to their table, which was decorated in the Swedish custom with Belgian and British flags. Every day they would each lower their flag and raise it again in a mock victory ceremony and the day was properly begun. They played table tennis, went for another run, had lunch and a sleep, went for yet another run, had a sauna and dinner, and talked and slept again.

Gosta Ollander marvelled at Dave's strength and worried about the elasticity of his muscles. Gaston took a delight in hiding Dave under beds and in dark corners when the occasional press man journeyed, for at least a day, to see him and there was no doubt in Gaston's mind where Dave would be at the end of the 10,000 metres in the European Championships in Helsinki—first. And so did I. At the time I wrote: 'Dave is in good shape, bodily and mentally. He has had enough of Valadalen and the edginess of the pre-race build up is beginning to show. Yet he is not too intense. On the way back from Valadalen, through the mountainous roads to the airport at Ostersund, he fell asleep as I drove a big Swedish Volvo at an average speed of sixty miles per hour. For myself, I would like him to think of the Helsinki race not as self-justification, or indeed as rehabilitation after the Crystal Palace débâcle, but simply as a dress rehearsal for the Olympics in Munich in 1972.' That was what I wrote at the end of the first week of August 1971. Three days later Dave was beaten out of sight in the European 10,000 metres by a virtually unknown Finn called Juha Vaatainen.

Towards the end of those championships I took Dave, and his current girl friend, out to dinner in Helsinki. He had suffered a tremendous shock to his pride and his self-esteem and yet it seemed to me little more than a problem of timing. He had been at his peak from the middle of June, when he had run the second fastest time in the world for the 5000 metres in Edinburgh, until the middle of July when he had run that electric 10,000 metres in Portsmouth. Now it was the middle of August and that inexplicable phenomenon which is known as 'staleness' had overtaken him. Staleness cannot be explained physically; it is just something that comes over the mind which somehow loses all joy, all life, in running. What I wanted to do over dinner was to persuade Dave to forgo the big cross country races of the winter (especially those abroad with all their awards) and to forgo the early season track races and to live for only one thing—the Olympic 10,000 metres final in Munich on September 3rd, 1972. I wanted to persuade him to deny himself all the transitory material rewards of a normal athletic season and to concentrate on the one thing that he wanted above all else in the world—an Olympic gold medal. I do not think I was successful. Perhaps there was too great a gulf between a young man of 21, to whom every day, every week, is of equal importance and a middle aged man of 42 who could look back on a span of life which has taught him that you can only achieve the ultimate if you cast all else aside and concentrate on one objective.

Yet the Gods seem to be on my side, for they interfered with his timing. In the late winter and spring of 1972, Dave was injured and his whole training programme was put back. He was not able to compete in the international cross championships, he was not able to produce those shattering times in May and June. It was not until the middle of July—only six weeks before his Olympic final—that he proved that he was fully fit again.

On Friday, July 14th, 1972, at the Crystal Palace the scene of the disaster the year before, he ran the fastest 5000 metres of the year. The next day, after only three hours sleep, he ran the fastest 10,000 metres in the world this year, leading from start to finish in his characteristic style, and leaving a talented field trailing three-quarters of a lap behind. Dave himself said there was no comparison between his fast runs in June and July 1971 and his fast runs in July 1972: 'the difference' he said 'is that last year I was tired of running by the time the AAA championships started. Now I am still fresh and eager to run.' Ron Clarke was there too and he said: 'I had already taken a bet in champagne that Dave will win the Olympic 10,000 metres before I heard about his 5000 metres last night. No, I don't think he will win the 5000 as well—that will go to Steve Prefontaine (USA)—but Dave will take the 10,000 metres. He has all my experience to learn from!'

The next day Dave once more escaped abroad, this time to Font Romeu, the high altitude training centre in the French Pyrenees. There he stayed for three weeks, with his rival Ian Stewart, trying to increase the haemaglobin content of his blood. I do not want to baffle you with too much medical science, and I am no expert in the physiology of the body, but it is important to understand the importance—or rather the supposed importance—of high altitude training for a modern long distance runner. So let me quote an expert: Dr. John Williams who wrote this in *The Guardian*:

'The higher one goes above sea level the thinner the air becomes. This means that each lungful of air at, say, 10,000 feet contains less of each of the normal constituents of the air we breathe (the *proportion* remains essentially the same) than a similar lungful at sea level. The same amount of oxygen is required to get a fixed amount of energy from your body, regardless of altitude. In the simplest terms this means that at altitude the heart and lungs have to work harder to provide the same amount of oxygen for the working muscles. If the heart and the lungs are already having to work flat out at sea level to provide enough oxygen for a given physical task, quite clearly they will not be able to provide enough at altitude, and the altitude performance will diminish. If you stay at altitude for several weeks a process of acclimatisation or adaption takes place to make the heart, lungs, and circulation more efficient—although the level of performance is not fully restored to that at sea level. The idea behind altitude training is that the acclimatisation changes which take place at altitude can help to improve the athlete's performance when he goes back to sea level, at least for 2 or 3 weeks.'

So that's why Dave—and Ian Stewart—went to the French Pyrenees. The honorary medical adviser of the British Olympic Association had sent a note to all the British teams in which he used words such as '. . . proved, beyond reasonable doubt, that for certain categories of competition there was likely to be an appreciable improvement on return to sea level after training at altitude'. So it was now the official policy of the British Olympic Association to offer altitude training to all those involved in continuous endurance events—and there is hardly an event that requires more continuous endurance than the 10,000 metres. So it is reasonable to say, is it not, that Dave was well advised to go to altitude? But let me quote Dr. John Williams again: 'The real place of altitude training in the preparation of sportsmen for competition has yet to be properly defined. It is certainly of value in the very few true "heart and lung events", e.g. the 10,000 metres run, but it is by no means the golden key to the winning of Olympic medals as some people claim, *while misused it may backfire disastrously*. From the British point of view it must always be remembered that altitude training means training abroad, with all the attendant risks of illness, home sickness, and staleness.'

What wise and prophetic words those turned out to be from a man who is one of the greatest experts that I know in the art of physical medicine and who is also Secretary General of the International Federation of Sports Medicine. Unfortunately, the British Olympic Association do not see fit to use his services because he is not a member of the 'old boy network' under which the British Olympic Association operates.

Dave and Ian returned from the Pyrenees at the end of the first week in August ready to run a mile at the Crystal Palace before flying off again, this time with all the other endurance event athletes for another session of altitude training at St. Moritz in the Swiss Alps. But neither Dave nor Ian were able to run that mile at the Crystal Palace because they had both caught a stomach bug in the Pyrenees and they needed to stay close to the dressing rooms and the facilities which they needed. But it did not seem to me to be anything to worry too much about. Surely in these days of modern medicine they could be cured within a day or two.

So Dave went to St. Moritz and ten days later I followed him across Europe to arrive, one brilliant morning, in a fairyland setting of high snow-covered peaks and lush valleys, sprinkled with azure lakes. There, in one of those soulless modern international hotels, the British athletic team—or rather all those athletes whose events meant that they had to run for longer than one and a half minutes—were encamped. It was not long before I learnt that Dave still had diarrhoea, but throughout the first week of his stay in St. Moritz it did not seem to worry him. He had been his usual big and bouncy self. As one member of the team put it: 'You couldn't fail to notice where he was. Where there was noise there was Dave.' He did not exactly endear himself to many other members of the British team because of the Cassius Clay-like impression that he conveyed of believing himself to be the greatest and everybody else a load of rubbish. It is an act born not of the certainty that he is the greatest but of a great lack of certainty, a lack of confidence.

Towards the end of the first week, on Saturday, August 12th, there was the now famous shooting incident. Dave, practising with his air rifle outside the hotel, swivelled around and let one off in the direction of the hotel. Accident or not, the shot passed uncomfortably close to Lachie Stewart (no relation to Ian but a great athlete in his own right, being the Commonwealth Games gold medallist in the 10,000 metres) and to Paul Nihill who share a room and a liking for Al Jolson records. More lack of endearment between Dave and other members of the team.

Next day, August 13th, Dave left with Ian Stewart on the long four-hour drive to Zurich from where they flew to Stockholm for a two-mile race the next day. Dave was going to break the world record. He said so. Indeed the world two-mile record was broken, but not by Dave—by a 23-year-old Finnish policeman called Lasse Viren. As usual Dave had led in the early stages but without his usual fire and rhythm and in the closing laps almost half the field swept by him, including Ian Stewart, and Dave could only finish sixth, an ignominious fourteen seconds behind Viren and two places behind Stewart. He came back to St. Moritz on Tuesday and he was a very different man—quiet and subdued. The worry, the lack of confidence, the realisation that his dreams of a gold medal might never be fulfilled was now inside him and running through his guts. He still had diarrhoea badly.

Some hours after I arrived I was talking to a doctor (who, because of medical etiquette, had best remain nameless) and I found him in a state of great anger because nobody responsible for Dave's health had taken a sample and had it tested to find out the real cause of Dave's gut trouble. Here was the most famous athlete in Britain, a boy of 22 who had captured the whole nation's imagination, and yet the organisation responsible for his health at this stage, the British Olympic Association, had not made arrangements for a sample to be tested. The doctor in St. Moritz thought it might be too time-consuming to arrange. And yet, as my doctor friend pointed out, it was essential to know whether there really was a bug or whether the whole thing was psychosomatic—a product of Dave's mental state.

Now let me make it quite clear that the doctors concerned with the British Olympic team are all nice men, and good at their jobs—like gynaecology and general practice. But there has not been, to my knowledge, any specialist in physical medicine, any specialist in stress physiology, any specialist in gastro-intestinal disorders, in any British Olympic team since 1952 which is when my experience starts.

So Dave's troubles persisted. He took a day off, playing golf and swimming, and then on Thursday afternoon, August 17th, he went down to the track in St. Moritz where he and his coach, Bob Parker, a 41-year-old coach builder in Park Royal, in north-west London, decided that he should run 8 × 300 metres—this is classical interval training and means that the athlete runs 300 metres fast and then repeats it eight times with only a short interval between each run. Unfortunately Dave and Bob Parker decided that Dave should run this session with Brendan Foster, who is the bronze medallist at 1500 metres in both the Commonwealth Games and the European Championships. It was a disastrous mistake—the end, I believe, of Dave's chances in the Olympics.

Every athlete, every member of the team, feels competitive against Bedford because Bedford is competitive against them. So this training session became a competitive session. Expert eyes could detect what was happening after the first 300 metres: Foster was going easily, Bedford was dragging a performance out of himself. But Parker still thought it was all right for Dave to continue. On the fifth repetition he blew up. He took off his spikes, put on his track suit and stalked off the track followed by Parker. It was at that badly timed moment that I arrived at the track and, not knowing what had just happened, I went across to talk to Dave. He thundered by without a word. Bob Parker said, apologetically: 'Not now, Chris.'

What a terrible week it had been for Dave: beaten decisively in

Stockholm, still troubled with diarrhoea and now destroyed in a training session. Is it any wonder that he cried that evening.

Back at the hotel, Ray Watson, a physiologist attached to the British athletes, took a blood test and found that Dave's haemoglobin (the iron pigment which carries oxygen to the muscles) was fantastically high—the second highest in the squad. Strangely enough, it was Brendan Foster who had the highest haemoglobin count. As Watson put it: 'Physically Dave is in marvellous shape. I believe he could run 27 minutes 15 seconds in Munich.' At the time the world record for the 10,000 metres was 27 minutes 39·4 seconds.

But Bedford was in mental turmoil. He felt under pressure and yet the only pressure there was had been created by himself: by the foolish shooting incident; by saying that he was going to Stockholm to break the world record; and by challenging another athlete over that athlete's normal training distance. The real problem, of course, was that Dave's dream of a gold medal in Munich was beginning to fade—all those years of training, training harder than any other distance runner in the world, did not seem to be enough. I believe that if there had been a British coach of real stature, someone like Geoff Dyson or Franz Stampfl, a man who could command Dave's respect, then that man could have helped him, could have pointed out all the positive things in his favour: could have told him that he had still run the distance faster than anyone else in the world; that most of the other athletes were frightened of him; that he had immense strength and vitality. But Dave does not get this sort of advice. Instead he fled from the scene. Jim Coote, who is the athletics correspondent of the *Daily Telegraph* and is also acknowledged to be Bedford's 'manager', drove him and Bob Parker down to Zurich to catch the night flight back to England.

All was peaceful in the team's hotel at St. Moritz because Denis Watts, the coach who was in charge of the team, had promised Dave to say nothing. But just before midnight all hell broke loose on the hotel's switchboard. Fleet Street had read the first edition of the *Daily Telegraph* in which there was a short front page story from Coote saying: 'With his coach Bob Parker he [Bedford] drove to Zurich where they hoped to find complete peace.' Coote, the journalist, had to send this story to his newspaper but Coote, Bedford's 'manager', should have kept quiet so that Dave could find the peace which he was seeking.

The hunt for Dave was now on. He shaved off his beard and moustache and slipped into London unnoticed, but of course the leader of the British athletic team, Arthur Gold, wanted to know where Dave was, and wanted to know how he was because if his health was really bad then there was still time to substitute another athlete in the 10,000 metres—someone like the young David Black who would have got into any other country's team. And back in St. Moritz we wondered whether he had any chance left of winning a medal in Munich. At the time I wrote: 'If he can get proper treatment in London; if he goes to a specialist who can really clear up his tummy trouble; if he can banish his own doubts and realise he is a great athlete who should not need constant reassurance, then anything is still possible.' But really in one's heart of hearts one knew that his Olympic hopes were destroyed. He was still physically a great athlete but gold medals are not won on physical ability alone and there was no doubt that there was not enough time—and nobody with the skill—to repair his mental state.

Sadly I too left St. Moritz and drove down through the long Engadine valley into Austria, over the Fern pass into Germany and along the autobahn into Munich.

2
'UNDER THE FLAG OF THE BOY SCOUTS'?

I cannot think what possessed me to drive straight to the Four Seasons hotel in the middle of Munich. It is normally a good rule to get yourself registered at the Press Centre, obtain all your passes, find your room and look for your communications: it is no good getting a good story and having no way of communicating it back to your newspaper. But for some inexplicable reason I went straight to the Four Seasons, the headquarters of the International Olympic Committee. And I walked straight into the Rhodesian row.

Now this is all a bit complicated and political, and it has very little to do with the athletes, so skip this chapter if you are not interested in the politics of sport. Unfortunately, these days, one just has to be interested in the politics of sport because they are getting more and more important and they control which athlete shall or shall not take part in the Games. Do not imagine that every athlete in the world is able to take part regardless of race, creed or politics as it says in the Olympic rules. No mainland Chinese athletes take part, for instance, because China refuses to join the Olympic movement while Formosa is allowed to remain in it—just like at the United Nations earlier this year when Formosa had to be chucked out before China would consent to join.

The situation at the Four Seasons was bad. It seemed possible that the African nations, a few of the Caribbean nations and many of the black American athletes would withdraw if Rhodesia took part, even though the African members of the International Committee had already agreed that Rhodesia could take part under certain conditions. Those conditions represented a slap in the face for Mr. Ian Smith and his illegal Rhodesian regime.

A year ago, at a meeting in Luxembourg, the International Olympic Committee had passed a resolution agreeing that Rhodesia could take part provided that the Rhodesians admitted, in effect, that the Unilateral Declaration of Independence had never taken place. Indeed, the resolution had been drafted by the African representatives with their tongues in their cheek because they never, for a moment, believed that Rhodesia would agree to:

1. Participate as a British colony.
2. Compete under the old colonial flag with the Union Jack in the corner.
3. Agree that 'God Save the Queen' would be their national anthem.
4. Agree that their nationality was that of a 'British subject'.

But sport is very important to the white minority of Rhodesia, just as it is important to the white minority in South Africa and the Rhodesian Olympic committee had agreed to all these conditions—presumably with a backing of Mr. Ian Smith's Government. So they had come to Munich with a mixed team of thirty athletes and they had done so without a passport. One of the most pleasant sidelines of the Olympic Games is that the host city has to get the agreement of its central government that all those people connected with the Games—athletes, officials and Press men—may travel to the city of the Games without a passport and without any visa. All they need is their Olympic identity card. And that is how the Rhodesians, whose passports are not recognised by any country which is a member of the United Nations, arrived in Munich. It was all according to the resolution passed in Luxembourg a year before, but now there were some African politicians—General Amin of Uganda amongst them—who did not like their presence at the Olympic Games.

So now we were faced with a complex political situation. We had already seen the odd spectacle of the Supreme Council for Sport in Africa—a supposedly non-political body—urging its members to take part in the Games alongside Rhodesia while the O.A.U. (Organisation for African Unity) was urging African nations to withdraw. Of course the two bodies had to get together and work out a common line, but the Supreme Council of Sport were worried by Avery Brundage's threat to investigate the independence of the

National Olympic Committees of Africa. Theoretically the National Olympic Committee of any country must be independent of its government and must be an entirely non-political body. It is good theory but in practice many National Olympic Committees depend on their governments for the money to send their teams to the Olympics. And if you take money from a government you can not be said to be truly independent of it. That evening, Sunday, August 20th, the representatives of the National Olympic Committees of Africa sat down and drafted a four-page resolution. It was a brilliant resolution. It reaffirmed the decision taken in Luxembourg the year before, and it latched on to three points in an effort to prove that the Rhodesian team had not complied with that resolution. The three points were that the Rhodesians had arrived in blazers with the single word Rhodesia on their pockets instead of 'Southern Rhodesia' as agreed; that their team had not proved that they were British subjects and that the head of the Southern Rhodesian delegation had flaunted the spirit of the Luxembourg agreement by declaring, on his arrival in Munich, that ' . . . we are ready to participate under any flag, be it the flag of the Boy Scouts or the Moscow flag. But everyone knows very well that we are Rhodesians and will always remain Rhodesians.'

The resolution went on to request 'the exclusion of the Southern Rhodesian team from the Games of the 20th Olympiad'. And the Africans threatened, that if Rhodesia was allowed to take part, then they would withdraw. It was not a situation that was going to be resolved that evening so I left them to it and drove north into the suburbs of Munich, to Olympia Park.

What an impressive place. What a monument to man, the builder! There is this huge stadium with its flowing glass roof erected at a cost of twenty million pounds for the roof alone; there are glass canopies swooping over the sports hall and the swimming bath down to an artificial lake. And behind it all a hill—an artificial hill made of the rubble from bomb-damaged Munich. Few cities in the world can have such a prime site so close to the centre of the city. It was, before and during the war, Munich's airport—as Croydon or Hendon had been the airports for London. Indeed, there is a historical connection between Hendon Airport and Olympia Park because it was from Hendon that Neville Chamberlain took off in 1938 to visit Hitler in his mountain hideaway in Berchtesgaden. And after that historic meeting Mr. Chamberlain, the British Prime Minister, took off from Olympia Park with the infamous 'Munich Agreement' in his pocket.

In the north-west segment of the old airfield was the Olympic village, and that is a misnomer if ever there was one. Does any village have more than 12,000 inhabitants? This one did, heaped one above the other in great concrete blocks. And the pipes that carry the heating and the water and the sewage are all exposed and designed to be a part of the ambience. There is even a stream in the middle of the concrete city which bubbles out of a concrete source and twists and turns, just like a natural stream, through marble banks, before falling down a concrete waterfall into a pool from which it is piped back up to its source again. And everywhere there are people, beautiful, supremely fit people and the babble of many tongues and it is all mightily impressive. But to me it was mightily oppressive. How on earth could you find anybody in this maze of concrete and pipes; how on earth was the Olympic spirit going to break through in such an artificial atmosphere?

It is just the same in the north-east corner of the old airfield which is known as the Press Centre. Six thousand of us are going to live here for four weeks, each in our little room stacked high into the sky like a mammoth battery farm. I do not know whether chickens still cluck when forced to live such an artificial life but I do know that there was a mighty clucking of a mighty number of journalists in this mighty housing estate from which the world was going to learn about the Games.

The Germans did their best. They tried to make it as friendly as possible and they only imposed four house rules, one of which read: 'The subsequent residents would be grateful if you did not remove or rearrange windows, doors or walls!' And they told us: 'Never fear, Golym's here!' Golym turned out to be a couple of computers into which every single fact about the Olympic Games had been fed and all you had to do was to ask one of the attractive German hostesses to punch Golym's keyboard and up he would come with the right answer. So as I went into dinner on that first evening, I thought I would ask him a simple question like how many medals the Finns had won between the wars in the 1500 metres, 5000 metres, 10,000 metres and 3000 metres steeplechase and would he please compare that with the number of medals that Finnish athletes have won in these events after the war. I took a long time over dinner, meeting old journalistic friends from Mexico and Tokyo and Rome and Melbourne and Helsinki and three hours later I went back for the answer. Golym was still at work and had now produced eighteen feet of paper—in duplicate of course—but he still had not finished. Somewhere in about the ninth foot of paper there was the name of the man who, so Golym said, had won the 1500 metres at the Berlin Olympics in 1936: Sten Suvio. This was a bit baffling as I seem to remember that that race was won by Jack Lovelock of New Zealand. Peter Wilson, the sports columnist of the *Daily Mirror* who covered the 1936 Games and who will be retiring after these Games, knew who Sten Suvio was—a boxing gold medallist! So much for the computers. Give me a man like Peter Wilson any day—a man who has not only seen it all and can remember it all, but can analyse it and place it in perspective. He is one of the very great sports journalists of this century and it will be a very sad day when we can no longer read his forecasts, reports and analyses.

But it is time that we went back to that Rhodesian situation. It took two full days of committees and councils for the inevitable to happen. Late on the afternoon of Tuesday, August 22nd, the International Olympic Committee took a vote and decided by 36 votes to 31, with three abstentions, to withdraw the invitation to Rhodesia to compete in the Munich Games. I have sometimes, indeed often, been sharply critical of Avery Brundage who has ruled over the International Olympic Committee for twenty years now. He is a millionaire and his money has isolated him from the realities of life but it has also given him a great independence which, allied with his own impregnable integrity, has allowed him to steer the Olympic movement through many crises and to hold out steadfastly against its exploitation by commercial interests and by politicians. But now he was defeated. He came into the Press conference, white in the face and with his arm on the shoulder of Monique Berlioux, the attractive Frenchwoman who was once a member of the French Olympic swimming team. He gave us the facts and then we asked for his opinion. He replied: 'Mr. Brundage ceases to officiate at this session and he prefers not to answer that question.' But under continued questioning he dropped this strange third person way of answering and when somebody said: 'Did he not find the political pressures growing with every Games?' he replied: 'I agree. The political pressures are now intolerable.' And then he walked out again, a sad, defeated man with his hand on Monique Berlioux's shoulder lest he should stumble.

Later, he let his feelings go and called it 'blackmail' and blackmail it was. Forty African nations had lined up against Southern Rhodesia and said 'Either they go or we go'. It was not a sporting contest—it was raw power politics played to maximum effect when the eyes of all the world were turned on Munich. Of course the Games will be a greater spectacle now that the Africans are staying and, if one wants to be nationalistic about it, there will also be less of a chance for British medals. If the African teams had gone they would have taken with them many athletes who are the greatest rivals of some of the British stars. John Akii-Bua of Uganda, for instance, is staying to do battle with David Hemery in the 400 metres hurdles; Kip Keino is staying to run the 1500 metres and perhaps the 10,000 metres against Dave Bedford. And Mamo Wolde of Ethiopia, the reigning marathon champion, is still in Munich to challenge Ron Hill. Of course the sport will be better, but what of the Olympic movement itself? Can it survive now that it has submitted to blackmail; now that its principles have been breached—especially the over-riding principle that men and women of all the world may compete regardless of their creed, their colour or their politics?

That night I did not find many people in Munich who believed that the Olympics could survive much longer. After all, it was politics and commercialism that killed the ancient Olympic Games of Greece and the same thing is happening to the modern Games.

And what of Mr. Brundage? He is a bitter, disappointed man. Many harsh things have been said about him—that he is out of touch; that, at 84 years old, he is too old; that it is easy for him, a millionaire, to be a pure amateur. But in these last three days he has won everyone's respect: an utterly honest man in a dishonest world.

It is worth reflecting for a moment on the power of the African nations. Twenty years ago no one would have cared a hoot whether they took part in the Games or not, for the simple reason that there were no good African athletes. Their people were too busy struggling for independence, for a roof over their heads and for enough food to fill their bellies. But then in 1960 a dark figure, bare feet whispering over ancient stone sets, came running down the Appian way in Rome, through the darkness, between two lines of flaming torches. Nobody knew who he was until he stopped running beneath the Arch of

Constantine in the floodlit shadow of the Coliseum. Then we learnt that his name was Abebe Bikila, that he was a member of the Emperor of Ethiopia's bodyguard and that he was the winner of the marathon—the first black African from an African country to win one of the prime events in the Olympic Games. Four years later, in Tokyo, he became the first ever man to win two Olympic marathon titles. Twelve years later he is here in Munich, in a wheelchair, a cripple for life, his spinal cord damaged in a car crash. But it was his performance in Rome in 1960, followed by that of Gammoudi in 1964 and the Kenyans in 1968, which conferred power on the African nations—power which they have used skilfully and ruthlessly here in Munich.

I can remember welcoming the arrival of this new sporting continent on the Olympic scene in 1960. Until that date the Olympic Games had been, in effect, a contest between the Americas, Europe and Australasia which meant that more than half the population of the world was barred from competing, either through want or subservience. Now, in 1972, more than half the population of the world is still barred through want or politics. Millions of people still have to use all their energies merely to feed themselves. China does not take part because of Formosa and Southern Africa is barred because of the policies of Vorster and Smith. Thus sport becomes a political weapon and a most powerful one when it means so much more than mere recreation and enjoyment.

I do not think we should be too smug about this, believing ourselves to be a mature, balanced nation. Just analyse your own feelings when watching any event on television; are you watching so that you can see experts perform supremely well, or is there a hint of nationalism, a feeling of pride or disappointment when a British athlete does well or badly? I would certainly like to meet the person who can truthfully deny that he or she does not transfer the victory of one of their fellow countrymen into some sort of warm feeling that all is still well in Britain.

I can remember being shocked as a young, naïve athlete at the Olympic Games in Helsinki in 1952 when I realised that the British public desperately wanted a British gold medal to give them some relief from austerity and recent rationing and convince them that we were winning the peace as we had won the war. When Roger Bannister, for instance, came fourth in those 1952 games instead of first, he was branded as a failure. In more recent times were there not some Labour politicians who firmly believed that they would not have lost the 1970 election if England's football team had not lost to West Germany in the World Cup? So let us face facts and realise that all the world, including ourselves, treats success or failure in sport as some sort of barometer—as a status symbol.

I do not like it, but then I do not like many of the things that are happening in sport these days. Yet it would be foolish to deny their presence. Frankly, I do not know what can be done about them. I know it is ridiculous to maintain the old amateur rules and expect any top sportsmen in any major sport to be able to do an ordinary job. I know that it is ridiculous to expect politics to be kept out of the Olympics, to expect that the International Olympic Committee can cut down on the size of the Games so that they are not restricted to the richest cities of the world. And because it is ridiculous to expect these things, I do not know how much longer the Olympic movement can continue. Its future now lies in the hands of an Irish peer, Lord Michael Killanin who has been elected to succeed Avery Brundage. At that election the votes were counted by a king—an ex-king of Greece—and by a Russian comrade. Indeed, the Olympic movement is a strange anachronism, trying to stand loftily above the materialism and politics of the world—standing for truth and honesty. But for how much longer?

3
'ALL THOSE FINELY TUNED MUSCLES'

Saturday, August 26th

I think it is time to start a 'Society for the Abolition of Olympic Games Opening Ceremonies'. But as opening ceremonies go—and you will gather that I am not one of their admirers—these Games have opened without a touch of militarism; without a hint of bombast; and without a sign of heavy Germanic grandeur.

But then we must remember that Bavarians are just about as untypical of what we British understand to be the German character as Venetians are of the whole of the Italian race. Bavarians treat life light-heartedly: in what other city, for instance, does the whole population indulge in a two-week-long drinking orgy known as the Oktoberfest? And they are not all that efficient. They can plan complicated operations and then carry them out (which is perhaps why they are so good at the complications of modern industry with its intricate production lines), but they are bad at improvising. When they bid for these Games six years ago, their idea was to prove to the world that Munich meant more than the city which spawned the Nazi movement—that they were in reality a city of people who have a relaxed and happy attitude to life. So they said that they would make these 'The Smiling Games' and they certainly did that today. Even the stadium itself is designed so that the flowing glass canopy smiles out over the Olympic site.

The only thing that will not bring a smile is the ache in the competitors' feet. Twenty years ago, in Helsinki, when I first took part in an opening ceremony, I can remember the tedium of the assembly, the ache of the march, the restlessness as one stood interminably in the middle of the stadium unable to see what was going on. And it was only relieved by one electric moment when Paavo Nurmi, probably the greatest athlete the world has ever seen, burst into the stadium carrying the Olympic torch. Today it must have been much more tiring for these thousands of competitors in a Games that is four times as big. Just imagine the feelings of an athlete: your muscles are tuned and supple for the coming fray and the nervous tension is beginning to rise in your body to manufacture the adrenalin which is so necessary to produce the greatest performance of your life. And then suddenly you are plunged into this charade; an early lunch before you put on your uniform (blue blazers and white flannels for the British) which is only fit for opening ceremonies, Government receptions or tea in a cricket pavilion. Then you have to file out of the village into the buses and wait, and wait, and wait until they fill up. Then the whole cavalcade moves off to the training grounds around the Olympic stadium and you get out of the buses and form up into teams with (if you are in the British team) the shortest at the front and the tallest at the back (the Americans do it the other way round so that the smallest girl is followed by a phalanx of men over seven feet tall!). And then you wait and wait until three o'clock when the first of the teams start to march into the stadium.

It took eighty minutes for them to march past because there are now 121 nations in these mammoth games. You can imagine what it does to all those finely tuned muscles, and imagine what the competitors think of the opening ceremony. But then it is all in aid of television so that the people of almost every country in the world can see that they are represented at this greatest of all sports festivals.

Certainly the teams were a fine sight: the Ethiopians, all in white with Mamo Wolde, the reigning Olympic champion gliding along in front with the Ethiopian flag and looking as fit to run that English distance of 26 miles 385 yards as any man I have ever seen. And then the strapping Australian girls looking extremely sunny. If the alphabetical order seems a little strange that is because German is a very strange language. Try identifying Elfenbeinkueste or Jungferninseln. The clue is that one is in Africa and the other in the Caribbean. The first is German for the Ivory Coast (how handsome all the Africans teams looked in their flowing, colourful robes) and the second is German for the Virgin Isles. From which one presumes that the German word for 'virgin' is 'Jungfern' which sounds rather charming.

The only touch of anxiety was a rumour that there might be a demonstration against some of the African nations because of the way they have tried to hound the Rhodesians out of Munich after their victory in getting them barred from the Games. But there was no sign of such a demonstration—instead it was rather touching to see the way the huge German crowd welcomed the East German team. No politics in it, just a roar of greeting to young men and women whose fathers and mothers were once of the same nation.

In all this kaleidoscope of colour it is the oddities that stand out: two grey haired men, apparently the entire team, from British Honduras. One was the team captain, the other the flag bearer. Perhaps they just came for the parade! And then there were the Canadians who have now established a tradition of turning out in the most vulgar outfits. Strangely enough their journalists wear it too. In Grenoble and Sapporo, Tokyo and Mexico their uniforms seared the eye. Here they were clad in red blazers, blue waistcoats and white trousers with white shirts with red spots. It might have been just all right—although on closer inspection, the spots were revealed as large red maple leaves—until one noticed that they also wore the most ridiculous white straw hat, in the shape of a Tyrolean hat, with a red artificial feather!

The British girls looked nice: handsome and smiling in their lilac dresses and white straw boaters. At the back of the British team was a separate contingent of yachtsmen looking very naval except for Rodney Pattisson, the gold medallist in Acapulco, who was once in the Navy but who has now left, presumably because they could not tolerate the length of his hair. He is the nearest thing there is to a certain gold medal in the entire British team.

But really it was two women who stole the show and one of them proved that the Americans are still expert at public relations. Who would they choose as their flag bearer—a white or a black athlete? It was the athletes themselves who decided that it should be Mrs. Hal Connolly who first competed in Melbourne in 1956—and won a gold medal—as Olga Fikotova of Czechoslovakia. There she started a fairy-tale romance with the American gold medalist in the hammer event, Hal Connolly. After much diplomatic brouhaha, Olga, the gold medallist from the Eastern bloc, married Hal, the gold medallist from the Western bloc. She is a big, handsome woman, strong enough to hold the American flag at arm's length just like the Russian wrestler holds the Hammer and Sickle. And the other woman was Chi Chen, extraordinarily beautiful and a great athlete. She too is married to an American but she comes from the Republic of China (Formosa) and she carried their flag, lithely, with her jet-black hair streaming down over her yellow dress. Alas, we shall not see her compete because she is injured.

When they were all in the stadium and lined up in serried ranks, three thousand Munich schoolchildren, dressed in yellow and blue and bearing garlands, encircled the teams and danced a welcome to a thirteenth-century English folk tune. That was an emotional moment—the youth of the host city welcoming all these great athletes from around the world. Then came the flame. Lit a month ago in the ancient ruins of Olympia and carried to Munich by a relay of nearly six thousand runners. And then the oath: 'In the name of all competitors I promise that we will take part in these Olympic Games, respecting and abiding by the rules which govern them, in the true spirit of sportsmanship, for the glory of sport and the honour of our teams.' Here emotion gave way to cynicism because one knew that the German athlete who took the oath on behalf of all the other competitors, the curvacious Heide Schuller, had had agents arranging for photographers to take her picture before the Games opened—on condition that the photographers paid for the privilege. And that is not entirely in keeping with the amateur spirit in which these Games are supposed to be held.

Tomorrow, however, we can forget all the politicking of the last few days, forget our cynicism, and revel in true competition between great athletes.

4
'BOYS DO NOT LIKE GIRLS WITH HUGE SHOULDERS'

Sunday, August 27th—Wednesday, August 30th

'They have a touch or feel with the water . . . they are at home in the aqueous element—everything they do progresses them through the water, every single movement is propelling them forward. It is impossible to develop. They either have it or not.'

Those were the words of the chief American swimming coach after Mark Spitz of the United States had won four individual gold medals and Roland Matthes of East Germany had won two. He was trying to explain two phenomenal athletes who are unbeatable in their chosen events. Mark Spitz, the good looking, dark haired, Californian American is now known in every house in the world that has a television set. Roland Matthes is not nearly as well known but is an equally fine swimmer. Four years ago in Mexico he won two gold medals—in the 100 metres and 200 metres back stroke—and here in Munich he repeated those wins thus totalling four individual gold medals—the same number of individual gold medals as Mark Spitz.

In the swimming pool they are very similar: their superiority is established the very second they hit the water and from that moment onwards nobody else has a chance against them. The water is their element and, as the American coach said, every movement of every muscle propels them forward. But out of the pool they are very different characters—as different as Western society is from Eastern society.

Roland Matthes is a product of the East German sports machine.

His talent was spotted when he was in a compulsory swimming lesson at school and from then on his coach has groomed him for Olympic stardom. He is still only 21 years old but a very mature, mild man who never seems to strain himself more than is necessary to make sure of victory. Several times he has been elected 'Sportsman of the Year' in East Germany—a title which Mark Spitz would never have won if there had been such an election in America. Indeed, Spitz is a complete contrast to Matthes out of the water. You might say that he is the Dave Bedford of American sport—an abrasive, apparently big-headed young man proclaiming to the world what he will win. Perhaps it would be more correct to say that that was what he was like before the 1968 Games but he has learnt better since then.

Before the Mexico Games in 1968 he made extravagant predictions about how many gold medals he would win. He had some justification for boasting because he did hold five American and three world records and he had won five gold medals in the Pan-American Games at Winnipeg in 1967. But the nearest he got to a gold medal in Mexico was a silver medal in the 100 metres butterfly and a bronze in the 100 metres free-style. It was nowhere near what his big mouth had predicted. He went home wounded and a little embittered, but back in the States he had the good fortune to come under the guidance of one of the most famous swimming coaches in the world, 'Doc' Counsilman at the University of Indiana. 'Doc' Counsilman took each member of the University team aside and quietly told them to forget everything they had read and heard about young Spitz and just to take him as they found him, an ordinary member of the team. Four years later a confident young man emerged, able to handle all the pressures, and he swept all before him. There is here a lesson for Dave Bedford except that I do not know who is going to be the 'Doc' Counsilman in Bedford's life.

On the first day of the swimming programme in Munich, Spitz won his first gold medal, the 200 metres butterfly, by more than ten feet—a very long way in a swimming pool. Later that night he anchored the American team to another victory in the 400 metres free-style relay and again it was a world record. So on his very first day in Olympic competition after his disasters in Mexico, Mark Spitz had two gold medals and two new world records. It was only a beginning.

Eight hundred miles north of Munich, in the Baltic port of Kiel, another great competitor was also making a beginning—Rodney

Pattisson. But while Mark Spitz has been improved and mellowed by Olympic competition, I am sorry to say that I believe that Rodney Pattisson has been soured. Four years ago Rodney was a 25-year-old Lieutenant in the Royal Navy—a pleasant blond young man who seemed to me to get immense enjoyment out of preparing his boat—which he called *Supercalifragilisticexpialidocious*—and sailing it with his friend Iain Macdonald-Smith. They prepared *Superdocious* with the greatest of care and they sailed her first over the line in six races out of seven. Like Mark Spitz here in Munich, it was a display of almost unparalleled superiority. But after the Mexico Games, Rodney and Iain split up and each went their own way.

Once again Rodney prepared his boat with extreme care—a new boat which he called *Supercalifragilisticexpialidoso*. But to me all the enjoyment seemed to have drained out of his life. The relaxed, pleasant personality has turned into a tense, excessively determined man who resigned his Naval career in order, apparently, to pursue one aim and one aim only—winning a second Olympic gold medal. He had arguments with officials, protested against decisions, fought a long battle with the controlling authority of the Flying Dutchman class and became so dedicated that many people began to fear what would happen to him when his competitive days were over. Sport after all is only one part of life and when it becomes everything to you, when every waking moment is spent in making yourself better at your one chosen event, then life becomes very narrow, very selfish. Nevertheless, one must admit that in Rodney's case it has worked. When the first race of the Olympic regatta was held in Kiel, Rodney and his new crew, Chris Davies, won the first race by a convincing margin.

It is worth looking at the set-up of the British yachting team in Kiel because they seem to me to be heading for more success than any other sport. Any sane betting man, who knows Olympic form, would bet against a British gold medal in the track and field events in Munich. But he would be insane to bet against a British gold medal from the British yachting team in Kiel. And that is not just because of the presence of the dedicated Rodney Pattisson; it is because the whole aura of the British team in Kiel smells of medals—gold, silver and bronze. The whole operation makes the rest of the world wonder what the hell has come over the British—gone are the old days of the weekend sailor and in their place has come a bunch of technical sailors who are entirely professional in their dedication to their sport. But let me turn to softer matters—to Shane Gould and Olga Korbut.

Shane Gould is a 15-year-old Australian schoolgirl from Sydney who is the fastest female free-style swimmer that the world has ever known—a girl who has broken records at every distance from a hundred metres to fifteen hundred metres. Here in Munich she is confidently expected to win four individual Gold Medals and the Australians are wrapping her in a cocoon to make certain nothing interferes with this objective. She is coached by Forbes Carlile who is the world's most famous coach of girl swimmers. He and his wife, Ursula, run a chain of training pools in Australia and it has become fashionable for Australian parents with promising children to send them to be tutored by the Carliles.

Forbes Carlile told my colleague David Hunn that Shane was not an outstanding physical specimen when she first came under his care, but the important thing was that she had the determination to apply herself to training—a regime which is almost a form of slavery. One of the apparent mysteries of sport is why the record breakers in swimming, particularly the girls, are so young. There is a very simple explanation.

In order to be a world class swimmer you have to devote hours every day to swimming up and down a pool, backwards and forwards, developing powerful shoulders and arms to pull yourself through the water. I have always believed that the main propulsion in swimming came from the legs but this is not so. Swimmers like Mark Spitz and Shane Gould can swim almost as fast with their legs tied together. They do not drive themselves through the water with their legs, instead they pull themselves through with their arms. After a time the tedium of this training and the fact that you develop massive shoulders and that your hair becomes streaked with green because of the chlorine in the water, affects a girl who discovers that boys do not like girls with huge shoulders and green streaky hair! So by the time a girl reaches the age of 16 she begins to revolt against this unnatural regime and then she ceases to break world records.

Shane did not win four individual gold medals and there were some people in the Australian team and the Australian press who thought that that was 'failure'. What a ridiculous word to apply to a girl who won three gold medals—in the 200 metres and 400 metres free-style and the 200 metres medley—and who also won a silver in the 800 metres and a bronze in the 100 metres free-style. Indeed, of the four individual free-style events Shane won a medal of one colour or another in all of them.

While Shane ploughed her way up and down the Olympic pool, another teenage girl was winning the hearts of everyone with her performances in the Sports Hall only a few yards away. Olga Korbut is two years older than Shane, but looks two years younger and about half the size. Olga is lucky to be competing at all: she came to Munich as one of the reserves for the Russian gymnastic team, but one of the other girls was ill and Olga, 17 years old, was given her chance. She is less than 5 feet tall, weighs only six stone and when you see her you wonder what a 12-year-old is doing in the Olympic Games. She looks like a child and has a child-like innocence which has captured the heart of the huge crowd in the Sports Hall in Munich and enchanted countless millions of television viewers across the world.

During the team competition, on Monday night, Olga made a complete hash of the start of her exercises on the asymmetrical bars and yet she went on to complete a performance that took the crowd's breath away. So two nights later when she had her second chance and came to perform her routines in the individual events, the crowd were determined that she was going to win a gold medal. They knew what they were doing because six years before during the World Gymnastic Championships in Dortmund, they kicked up such a racket that the judges were forced to raise the mark which they had given to one of the competitors—an American girl called Doris Fuchs.

Here in Munich the crowd tried to do the same again. They did not like the marks which Olga had been given for her performance on the asymmetrical bars, so for a full ten minutes they howled and whistled in derision. So when the gymnasts moved on to the next apparatus—the beam—the judges seemed to be a little afraid of the crowd's reaction if they were anything less than generous to the young Russian girl. It was utterly unfair, yet understandable, and after the beam exercises were completed and Olga had just beaten her 18-year-old team mate Tamara Lazakovitch, the television cameras revealed a look of utter disgust on the face of Miss Lazakovitch. But to me there was no doubt that Olga did deserve her gold medal and also the second gold which she won in the floor exercises.

How do you describe enchantment? Anyone who has seen Olga in the flesh or on television knows that she has an indefinable quality —perhaps best described as abandonment to the joy of life—which entirely captures people's hearts.

She is still a schoolgirl. Her father is an engineer and her mother a cook and she comes from a small town in White Russia called Grobno, near Minsk. For a 17-year-old, she is tiny and very undeveloped but that is one of the reasons why she is determined that she has to excel in something—at school she was always the smallest child in her class and this worried her and made her determined to do well in something. Perhaps, in any other country she would have gone unnoticed but not in Russia where every potential Olympic athlete is spotted and passed on to a coach who can develop their full potential. Olga came under the influence of a man called Renald Knysch who had trained one of the Russian gold medal winning teams of 1964—the team which Olga saw on television, a decisive moment in her life because it was then, while watching the Russian girls perform in the Olympics of 1964, that Olga decided that she too would be a gymnast.

It was Renald Knysch who developed Olga into something entirely new in the world of gymnastics. She is not in the classical flowing Russian tradition—indeed she is almost American in some of her movements, like those puppet movements she makes during her floor exercises. I find that she has the same affect on my emotions as the young American ice skater Janet Lynn who competed in the Winter Games in Sapporo in February.

Personally, I believe that Janet Lynn is the greater performer of the two because she combines the maturity of a woman with this abandonment of a child. Yet Janet never won a gold medal in Sapporo because there is no equality in the Olympics. A gymnast like Olga has the opportunity of winning five individual gold medals (the beam, the asymmetrical bars, the horse vault, the floor exercises and the combined exercises) and one team gold medal, whereas an ice skater only has the chance of one gold medal awarded for her combined score in the compulsory figures and the free skating—two very different types of event which require very different skills.

Yet gold medal or no gold medal Janet Lynn, who is 5 foot 2 inches tall, weighs 8 stone 10 pounds and is 18 years old, has the ability to sear your soul. She is very blonde with her hair cut in urchin style, has a strong chin and a freckled nose and she is, according to Otto Lang, the best free skater since Sonja Henie. Otto Lang should know because he was the man who advised Hollywood on the winter sports sequences in all those Sonja Henie films. Janet's performance in Sapporo when she got the top marks in the free skating (but of course no gold medal) was one of those rare occasions when sport is lifted into the realms of art.

What she did on the ice has a number of technical names: one foot axel, reverse jump, double axel, half loop, reverse jump, inside axel and double loop. But if you describe her performance in these technical terms it would be like trying to analyse someone in love by the changes in their body chemistry. All that the spectator saw in Sapporo was a small person conveying something great to the audience. And that something is, I believe, a love of life.

It would be very easy to believe that Miss Lynn is too good to be true. I can remember asking her what she did on the day of her competition in Sapporo and she said: 'I prayed a lot, I asked God to give me the right feeling. When I got out on to the ice I just tried to enjoy myself, to give everything I had got—not to give up for one second.'

There is sometimes an honesty about an athlete talking that may make them sound self-righteous, boastful and unworldly but there is nothing self-righteous or boastful about Janet Lynn. She is unworldly if you believe the world to be a hard and often cynical place, and so I fear for what will happen to her when the world grabs her. And the world will want to grab her because she could be made into a Hollywood star.

She lives in the mid-west of America in Rochford, Illinois, where her father keeps a drugstore. She started skating on the frozen ponds around her home when she was 2½ years old and she so obviously enjoyed it that her parents arranged for her to have lessons, just as many small girls in Britain might go to dancing class. Her teacher, a Czech, Mrs. Slavka Kohout, was one of those people who often make the best coaches—someone who might have been really good themselves if circumstances had been right. Mrs. Kohout, as a girl, had been Mid-West champion and then her father died and she had to give up skating in order to earn some money. It is easy to say that such a person coaches in order to live vicariously, basking in the success of their protégés, but it is more subtle than that. They were never able to bring out the best in themselves so they retain their enthusiasm for bringing out the best in others.

At the age of 11 Janet started to skate competitively and by the age of 14 she was competing in the 1968 Winter Olympics in Grenoble where she finished ninth—higher than Sonja Henie's first appearance at the age of 12 in the Games of 1924. After Janet had won a bronze medal in Sapporo and had been acclaimed as the greatest free skater in the world, she was rather confused. People were beginning to want part of her, to demand her time, but all she knew was that she wanted to keep on skating: 'Until I do not want to skate any more—and I cannot think that will ever happen.'

There was a movement in that programme in which she skated in Sapporo when she suddenly moved backwards so that her blonde hair flew forwards and her arms were outstretched and she was indeed a young girl in love with the world. But she would say that all she is doing is thanking God for so much happiness. Those of us who watched her can make of it what we will, knowing only that it was supremely beautiful.

It is not often that one sees the same magical moment twice in one year but here it was again in Munich in the person of Olga Korbut. She and Janet seem to me to be the embodiment of the Olympic spirit. Perhaps I am too romantic, but to me they symbolise a freedom of spirit and an utter mastery of their sport which has nothing to do with worldly possessions or politics or national status. They are, very simply, two young girls doing something extremely well and doing it with their hearts as well as their bodies.

And yet what will the world make of them? Will it see them as representatives of two different ideologies; Russia and America; Communism and Capitalism? Will it see them as two valuable properties to be exploited? Or will it see them—as I hope it will—as two ordinary girls who have devoted a part of their childhood to learning to do something supremely well and who will want to put this aside and go on to do all the other things that there are in life?

* * *

These first four days of the Olympics are very diffuse. Events are taking place all over Munich, most of them heats and preliminaries, and there is no centre to the Games because the stars of the Games, the track and field athletes, have not yet taken to their stage in the

Olympic Stadium. So let us take a swing round the various sites and see what is going on.

Northwards from Munich, past some vast housing estates and an old military airfield, in a place called Hockbruck, is a brand new shooting complex which cost £3 million to build and which has facilities for two thousand spectators. It certainly is the oddest spectator sport I have ever seen. If you have an exceedingly powerful pair of binoculars you can just detect the squeeze of a competitor's finger on the trigger and if you have a powerful telescope you can pick out the small hole that the shot makes. If that is what watching sport is about then you can count me out.

But even at Hockbruck funny things happen. Ho Jun Li is a 26 year-old soldier in the North Korean army and on Monday, August 28th, he won the Small Bore Rifle Prone (which means lying down) shooting event with the incredible total of 599 points out of a possible 600 and he did it because he thought that 'I was aiming at my enemies. Our Prime Minister told us prior to our departure to the Olympics to shoot as if we were fighting our enemies,' and this is exactly what he did. This created a great fluttering of anxiety amongst the Organizing Committee, one of whom said: 'This is most embarrassing. The other teams are angry and demanding an official apology.' So the North Koreans hastily called another press conference at which Li said that he had been misquoted.

The next day it was a British official who, so the British team said, had been misquoted. Jim Fox, a 30-year-old soldier from Portsmouth who has been the British modern pentathlon champion for seven years, was unexpectedly leading after the first two days of this event which is based on an old military fable. The modern pentathlon consists of riding, fencing, shooting, swimming and running—the idea being that a soldier is sent off from the front line with an urgent message. His horse gets shot from under him so he defends himself with his sword (it is an old style war this); then he fights off more enemies with his pistol before swimming across a river and running the rest of the way to headquarters!

After the riding and the fencing, Jim Fox was unbelievably in the lead but then came pistol shooting, which is his weakest event. The problem is to control your nerves. In normal training most good competitors can score well over 190 out of a possible 200 with the rapid fire pistol over 25 metres but when it comes to Olympic competition, nerves start to affect your eye and hand. In Mexico four years ago some of the Swedish competitors steadied their nerves with a drink or two and got disqualified because alcohol is a drug. Here in Munich some of the competitors seem to have found another method of calming their nerves which led Monty Mortimore, the British pentathlon team manager, to claim that some of the teams were so expert at administering certain doses of drugs that they were able to beat the antidope squad: 'I am not saying they used stimulants, but it is unbelievable that any competitor could shoot like I saw today without the use of a needle of some sort. One of the Russian competitors who stood next to Jim Fox was remarkably relaxed. . . .'

As soon as this statement reached the Olympic Village the British team chief, Sandy Duncan, issued a statement expressing: 'Deep regret to the countries concerned that such unsubstantiated accusations should ever have been made.' Maybe Monty Mortimore ought to have kept his mouth shut and have gone to the Organizing Committee but he was certainly proved to be right in the end. The Medical Commission of the I.O.C. announced that they had found traces of tranquillisers in fourteen of the Modern Pentathalon competitors, but they were not going to disqualify them because tranquillisers were not yet on the list of prohibited drugs.

Some thirty miles to the west of Munich there is another incredible Olympic site at Augsburg, where £2 million have been spent on constructing an artificial river for the canoe slalom. A year ago the East Germans came and studied this artificial river and built a duplicate in East Germany so it is not very surprising that they carried off most of the medals much to the chagrin of the West Germans who have not yet won a single gold medal. One of their newspapers carried a banner headline: 'East Germany wins the medals but we keep smiling.'

While all this varied activity has been taking place on the competition sites, Dave Bedford has hit the headlines again. He's been summoned before the I.O.C. Elegibility Committee to answer a charge that he allowed his name to be used in connection with advertising, thus infringing the amateur code. Indeed, there are two parts to the charge: the first is that a Belgian newspaper used a picture of him wearing a T-shirt displaying the name of a sport goods firm: and the second is that he allowed the *Sun* newspaper to advertise his exclusive story. To use legal phraseology, the charge was returnable at 9.30 in the evening in the palatial Four Seasons hotel. We all hurried down there and hung about in the lobby. At 10.15 p.m. Dave emerged from the committee room in company with Sandy Duncan, the chief of the British team, and Arthur Gold, the British athletic team manager. The television lights blasted into their faces and Sandy told us that Dave had been cleared on both charges. But it is hardly the best preparation for running the greatest 10,000 metres of his life.

5
'IS THIS A REPLAY OF THE HEATS?'

Thursday, August 31st

Last night on BBC television I was talking about the most hazardous occupation that I know—forecasting Olympic track and field results. I recalled the 1952 Games in Helsinki when Roger Bannister was a hot favourite for the 1500 metres. The night before the final I talked over the field with Roger, analysing the strengths and weaknesses of every one of his opponents. We came to the name of Jose Barthel of Luxembourg, a man I had run against. I was quite confident: 'I doubt very much if he will be with you with 300 metres to go,' I told Roger, 'and if he is then you can forget about his finish—he hasn't got one.' Well, Jose Barthel was with Roger—in front of Roger—with 300 metres to go and he sprinted away to become the gold medallist with Roger in fourth place.

And then I recalled the 1964 Games in Tokyo when Ron Clarke, the man with the fastest time in the 10,000 metres field, was in the lead with only four laps to go and had already dropped all his leading contenders. Ron looked around and saw three unknown athletes hanging on grimly—an American Red Indian, a Tunisian army sergeant and a member of the Emperor of Ethiopia's bodyguard. At that moment every expert in the stadium had already awarded Ron the gold medal. But it was the American Red Indian, Billy Mills who won the gold and the Tunisian army sergeant, Mohamed Gammoudi, who won the silver. So you soon learn that in the Olympics it does not pay to write anyone off. They have all trained, every one of them, through heat and cold, tropical thunderstorm and arctic sleet, for year after year, for this one day in their life, and nobody's reputation is going to frighten them.

But who would have forecast what happened—or rather did not happen—in the Olympic stadium today on the first day of the track and field programme. The Americans have the fastest sprinters in the world—they have won the 100 metres title twelve times in sixteen Games. Since 1932 only Armin Hary (of Germany) has broken the American dominance. But to win an Olympic title you must arrive at the starting line on time! This morning the three American sprinters, Eddie Hart, Rey Robinson and Bob Taylor came comfortably through the first round. Then came the second round at 4.15 in the afternoon and as the competitors went to their blocks there was no sign of the three Americans. As we learnt later they were standing at a bus stop outside the Olympic television centre waiting for transport to the stadium and they were looking in through the open door of one of the control suites. They saw a 100 metres race being won. 'Is this a replay of the heats?' they asked an engineer. 'No, that's live,' was the reply and they realised that they should be taking part. They dashed to the stadium but only Bob Taylor arrived in time for his race.

You can imagine the furore in the American camp. A post-mortem revealed that Stan Wright, the assistant coach in charge of the sprinters had read 16.15 hours as 6.15 p.m.—a very costly mistake.

But, of course, the event that we had all been waiting for was the 10,000 metres heats, and they were certainly sensational. Dave Bedford was in the first heat in company with the reigning champion, Naftali Temu of Kenya, and Emile Puttemans of Belgium who once held the world two mile record. On the top corner of the track ther was a loud British contingent of supporters waving the Union Jack and they soon had something to shout about when Dave went to the front in his characteristic manner just as he passed in front of them after one lap.

He certainly put his rivals on the rack, did Dave. Gradually, one by one, the field dropped away until, after sixteen laps, Dave and the Belgian, Emile Puttemans, were on their own and lapping Temu. On and on went Dave and Emile, drawing further and further ahead and making it look all so easy. With 500 metres to go they started talking to each other as if neither was quite certain how many more laps were left. It seemed to me that Dave wanted to run in easily but the Belgian of the flowing stride would have none of it and in the last twenty yards he proved to Dave that if it was to come to a sprint in the final then he was the better man. The time (27 min 53·4 sec for Puttemans and 27 min 53·6 sec for Bedford) was a new Olympic record, beating Billy Mills' time in Tokyo by more than half a minute. But then the Olympic record in all the distance events is somewhat false because there was no opportunity for anybody to break distance records in the rarefied air of Mexico in 1968.

A Finnish journalist said to me afterwards: 'Dave is good and that is bad for us'—meaning, of course, that Dave looks fit to run the race of his life in the final on Sunday against the Finnish favourite Lasse Viren. But what extravagance Dave showed. I was always told to qualify for the final by using the minimum amount of energy while at the same time making certain that I did qualify. Dave and Emiel had smashed the field by the halfway mark and could have taken the second half of the race very easily. Yet they still kept up an unbelievable pace. They went through the 5000 metres mark faster than that world record-breaking run by Chris Chataway and Vladimir Kuts at the White City in 1954. And then they ran another 4600 metres and started chatting! That was real gamesmanship—each trying to prove to the other that really it was so easy.

The other two heats were won by Mohamed Gammoudi of Tunisia in 27 min 54·8 sec and Merus Yifter of Ethiopia in 28 min 18·2 sec. I must confess that I had never heard of Mr. Yifter when I arrived in Munich but some experts whose judgement I respect warned me that he was a man to watch. He is small and stocky—rather like Kuts or Chataway—and looks immensely strong. Others who caught my eye were the tall mustachioed American Frank Shorter and the slight figure of the Finnish runner Lasse Viren, both running in the same heat as Gammoudi. But, of course, the real sadness of the day was to see Temu lapped—Temu is the man who stopped the greatest distance runner of all time, Ron Clarke, from winning gold medals in the Commonwealth Games in 1966 and the Olympic Games in 1968. Truly, the standard of running in the heats today is utterly unbelievable.

It is so tough that neither Lachie Stewart, the Commonwealth Games gold medallist, nor Dave Holt, was able to qualify for the final. It is not unexpected in the case of Dave Holt because he is the most surprising member of the British track team. He is one of hundreds of competent British cross-country runners who train hard and thoroughly enjoy their sport. But few of them ever get international recognition. Indeed Dave, a 28-year-old civil servant, was not even considered good enough to be put into the 'A' race in the A.A.A. championships which acted as the final Olympic trials. So he stood on the starting line at the Crystal Palace and refused to be moved. How right he was. He ran the race of his life to come third to Dave Bedford and Lachie Stewart and thus win his place in the Olympic team—an example to all those athletes who keep plodding away over the country in the winter.

Nobody really expected him to qualify for the Olympic final and he ran competently enough to come eleventh in Gammoudi's heat with a time of 28 min 46·8 sec. But I wonder what happened to Lachie Stewart? He was sixth in Yifter's heat in a time of 28 min 31·4 sec which is well outside his best—28 min 11·8 sec when he won the Commonwealth title in Edinburgh in 1970. Lachie told me in St. Moritz that he had never been fitter, so I am beginning to wonder about the effectiveness of altitude training. Indeed, it seems that Dr. John Williams may be right when he says that it causes more disturbance than benefit, particularly for those athletes who have not tried it before.

The standard in the women's 800 metres was equally unbelievable. Do you remember Ann Packer winning the 800 metres in 1964 in Tokyo with a new Olympic record of 2 min 1·1 sec. Today that time would have only got her third place in one of the *heats*. Only one of the five heats was won in a time slower than 2 min 2·0 sec and one of them, the second, was won by the slight Bulgarian girl, Svetlana Zlateva, in the exceptional time of 1 min 58·9 sec, which is only two-fifths of a second outside the world record set by the blonde German girl Hildegarde Falck in 1971. In this class of competition only one of the British girls, Rosemary Stirling, qualified for the semi-final. She ran 2 min 3·6 sec to come third in the fifth heat. And Pat Cropper (more familiarly known as Pat Lowe before she married Dave Cropper) ran the same time in the fourth heat but could only come fourth and that was not good enough. Margaret Coomber ran even faster—2 min 3·0 sec in the third heat but so fierce was the competition that it was only good enough for sixth place.

Of the other British athletes, Dave Hemery looked very powerful in winning his heat of the 400 metres hurdles in 49·72 sec—the fastest time of the day. But Paul Nihill, who felt so confident of getting a medal in the 20 kilometres walk—a distance which he has walked faster than anyone else in the world—could only come sixth. This event, which is traditionally the first gold medal to be won in the stadium, has always set the tone for the British team. If a British walker does well then the rest of the British team do well throughout the Games. Today Paul did exactly as he had planned—going to the front after 12 kilometres (7½ miles) and then trying to walk away from the opposition. He went to the front all right but he could not walk away from the opposition. Indeed, he only held the lead for about fifty yards when his legs started to feel very heavy. 'It may be that I came down from altitude too late,' he said afterwards. Or it may be that altitude training, as advised by the medical officers of the British Olympic Association, is a lousy idea.

Perhaps the biggest tragedy of the day for the British team was John Sherwood who won the bronze medal in Mexico behind David Hemery in the 400 metres hurdles. Early this morning in the heats he pulled a muscle when going over the third hurdle and all his long months of training have come to naught. He pulled up, staggered off the track clutching his leg, and sank his head into his hands. From the long jump pit came his wife Sheila who had been qualifying for the long jump final. She wrapped her arms round her husband and they crouched there, silent in their misery. John Sherwood's Olympics had lasted for precisely fourteen seconds.

Elsewhere in Munich, Jim Fox ran the last event of the Modern Pentathlon—the 4000 metres cross-country run—with great courage to record the fastest time of 12 min 35·0 sec but, after his disastrous performance in the shooting events, today's run was only good enough to raise him from eighth to fourth place, just outside the medals. I wonder how many of those in front of him had won their medals because they took tranquillisers in the shooting event? Well though he ran today Fox has always seemed to me to be content to settle for a good place instead of a medal. All through the tournament he has said that he would be happy to improve on his eighth place in the Mexico Olympics. Twice he has come fifth in the world championships, so today's performance is his best ever. Nevertheless, one has the feeling that if he had more confidence in himself, he might have done still better.

Before the athletics started in the main stadium I drove out to the little village of Poing where the Three Day Event was being held. This event, known as 'the Military Event' in Germany, consists of three separate parts: the dressage, which is a complicated series of movements to prove the obedience and balance of a horse; the endurance test which is itself divided into four parts—just over 2 miles of road and track which has to be ridden in a minimum of 15 minutes and is, therefore, nothing but a warm-up; the steeplechase which again is just over 2 miles and incorporates a number of simple obstacles; another section of roads and tracks, some 15 kilometres in length (just under 10 miles) which has to be ridden in 63 minutes (there is nothing very severe about that); and then the cross-country stage. This is the heart of the event. The competitor has to ride over 8 kilometres (5 miles) and negotiate thirty-six complicated and ferocious obstacles, some of which are enough to scare the most courageous rider.

But it is hardly a spectator event. I spent most of the morning there, walking long distances in the blazing sunshine and saw about ten competitors jump three of the obstacles. I had to leave for the main stadium before Richard Meade rode the course with a brilliant clear round in the fastest time of the day, thus putting him in line for the individual gold medal and the British team in a good position for the team medal. Tomorrow, if all their horses pass the veterinary inspection, they will have to ride a comparatively simple jumping course; and if Richard Meade and his horse Laurieston can have a clear round then they will win the first British gold medal of the Games.

6
'JUST BEHIND MEADE WAS A GIRL, SMILING'

Friday, September 1st

Let me start at the back end of the day. It was nearly midnight when I took Dave Starbrook, who is Cockney to the core and had a silver medal dangling round his neck, and Ray Ross, the British Judo team manager and coach, out for a beer and a pizza when we paused at the door of the television building to let a delegation through that somehow conveyed a sense of importance.

Indeed, they were rather important. The man in front was in a dinner jacket and very handsome—Richard Meade, who had just won two gold medals in the Three Day Event. Just behind Meade was a girl, smiling—a rather embarrassed smile—at the orange-suited men who control admission to the building. It was, indeed, Princess Anne. Two worlds met at that moment.

Princess Anne's world and that of Richard Meade—the upper crust, Hickey-column world—is well known even if it is utterly outside our own experience. The world of Dave Starbrook, the first British sportsman ever to win a Judo Olympic medal, is easier to imagine. Every day he gets up just after six and opens up his newspaper, tobacco and sweet shop in Wells Road, Hackney. He does everything himself—the early sorting of newspapers, the morning rush hour for cigarettes, the lunch time rush hour for sweets. He does not shut up shop until 6.30 p.m. That happens for six days of the week and the seventh day he takes it easier, opening up the shop for a mere six hours from 8.00 a.m. until 2.00 p.m. Every weekday evening after he has shut up shop he travels to Regents Park, to his Judo club, Renshoden, and trains. At the end of the day he is, to use his own word, "knackered'. It has cost him, he estimates, about £250 to compete here in Munich—that includes his own loss of wages, payment to someone to look after the shop, and his training expenses throughout the year. 'Married?' he says, 'Of course not. I can't afford it.'

But it will all be worth it if it puts his beloved sport in front of the British public and makes them realise what a great sport it is—especially for children. That I can testify to because I have a 8-year-old son who is nuts about it. He goes to a class every Saturday morning and then comes home and tumbles around the garden doing those neat crossed leg rolls which break a fall—'ukimy' in the jargon of Judo.

Dave Starbrook fought throughout a long afternoon and evening. He was very calm and used all his tremendous strength to take him to the final where he lost a close decision to the Russian, Shota Chochoshvili, who won with what is known in the Judo business as a 'sogogachi'. I give Dave pride of place on this day, even although he won a silver medal and not two gold medals like Richard Meade. That is because Judo is a universal sport which almost anybody can take up: Unlike the Three Day Event which requires you to be a rich man or woman. Indeed, there cannot be as many Three Day Event competitors in the whole world as there are Judo practitioners in Britain.

But having said that let me give due credit to Richard Meade who completed the Three Day Event with a faultless round in the show jumping ring at Reim this afternoon. And he led the team of Mary Gordon-Watson on Cornishman V, Mark Phillips on Great Ovation and Bridget Parker on Cornish Gold to a team victory and a second gold medal—only one gold medal between the four of them but then this team event is a bit of a farce. Of course there are team events in other sports in the Olympics but they are always kept separate from the individual events. For instance, a swimmer like Mark Spitz has to swim again in the relay before winning another gold medal but in the Three Day Event the scores of the three best riders from any nation are added together and then a medal awarded to all four riders of the leading nation. It really is nonsense. In the marathon, for instance, Britain would have won the team medal many, many times if one had been awarded. It should be a good principle that you cannot get two medals for the same performance but, as always, the International Olympic Committee have compromised and allowed the International Equestrian Federation—whose President is Prince Philip—to award one medal to the four competitors (and their horses).

Prince Philip was there to see Richard Meade win and so was Princess Anne whose name has often been linked romantically—as they say in the gossip columns—with Richard Meade.

Over in the Olympic stadium a 22-year-old Russian from Kiev, Valeri Borzov, became the fastest man in the world. This well-built man, with incredibly powerful thighs, is one of the finest sprinters I have seen—matched only by the huge black American Bob Hayes who won the 100 metre dash in Tokyo in 1964. But what a contrast between these two: Hayes was the most forceful sprinter I have ever seen, using brute strength to propel him down the track: but Borzov is the smoothest, most balanced sprinter I have ever seen. He has one fault. He will always turn his head just before the tape to make certain that he has won and that could be fatal if there was anyone to match his talent.

In the Press conference afterwards some American journalists asked him: 'Don't you think that you're only the fastest man in the world on paper?' Presumably they meant to imply that one of the two Americans who failed to get to the starting line in the second round heat yesterday would have beaten Borzov today. But I just don't believe it. Borzov has been over to America and beaten American sprinters on their home ground and so there is no earthly reason why he should not have done the same on neutral ground here in Munich. Besides, there are some good judges of American sprinting form who think that Bob Taylor, who came second to Borzov today, is the best of the American trio.

David Hemery moved smoothly into the final of the 400 metres hurdles but the threat of John Akii-Bua has been revealed. There was some extremely stupid seeding in the semi-finals with the three most fancied athletes—David Hemery, John Akii-Bua of Uganda, and Ralph Mann of the United States—being drawn together in the first semi-final. And it was John Akii-Bua who won with a time of 49·23 sec, with Ralph Mann second in 49·53 sec and David Hemery third in 49·66 sec. These placings do not worry me because this, after all, was a semi-final, but what does worry me is the scene just after they had passed the winning post: Dave was crouched on the ground trying to get some air back into his lungs while Akii-Bua stepped lightly over another hurdle and then shot his feet out once or twice in that hurdling movement just to remind them of what they have to do tomorrow.

Semi-finals can be very deceptive things because you cannot see into a man's mind. How much was Dave holding back? How much of his nervous energy was he storing up? One heck of a lot I believe. He only came third in his semi-final in Mexico four years ago and yet the next day he showed such superiority, such complete mastery, that he will go down in Olympic history as one of those very special gold medallists in the class of Emil Zatopek, Jesse Owens and Bob Hayes. Nobody, for instance, had got anywhere near Dave's world record—48·1 sec set in Mexico—but I believe someone will tomorrow and I hope it will be Dave.

I cannot help being impressed by the strength of these Africans. Not only John Akii-Bua but also Robert Ouko and Mike Boit, both of Kenya, who each won their second round heats in the 800 metres. Andy Carter ran a very courageous race in Boit's heat. He knew that it was possible that he would not be in the first two (who were the only certain ones to qualify) so he made a very fast pace and was only overtaken in the last few yards by Mike Boit and the impressive Russian Evgeni Arzhanov. Andy's time, 1 min 46·3 sec, was fast enough for him to qualify as one of the two 'fastest losers'.

The third heat in the 800 metres was an absolute classic. Dave Wottle of the United States came to Munich with an injured leg and with a brand new wife to spend his honeymoon running in the Olympic Games and he really does not seem to be able to summon up much interest in the proceedings in the stadium! When the gun goes off he is caught dithering on the line and by the time the field has gone 200 metres Dave, wearing a ridiculous, and rather dirty, white golf cap, is about twenty yards behind the leaders. And a lap later when there's only the final bend and the final straight left he is still at the back of the queue and boxed in. But come the finishing straight and he slides smoothly through on the inside. On television tonight I called him 'The Head Waiter', because he seems to run a race just like that famous jockey, Harry Wragg, rode a race. I went further and said that his performance today was the most masterly display of tactics that I have ever seen. But that was before I talked to Dave and discovered that he does not really know what he is doing!

It was very sad for me to see no British representatives left in the steeplechase—my own event. In the various heats Andy Holden came fifth, John Bicourt eighth and Steve Collins fourth. The final, which will be run on Monday, looks like a carve up between three Finns and three Kenyans with the whole of the rest of the world filling the remaining six places. What a contrast there is between the smooth technique of the Finns and the way that the Kenyans—particularly Kip Keino—hubble and bubble over each obstacle. But these Africans have the strength to do it and that is one of the most vital ingredients in a modern athlete.

7
'I AM ONE OF FORTY-THREE FAMILIES'

Saturday, September 2nd

Neither David Hemery nor Ralph Mann needed any comfort—they knew they had lost the 400 metres hurdles final to an incredible athlete, John Akii-Bua, who says that he comes from a family of forty-three children!

But poor Dave Wottle who won the 800 metres in the very last stride had to be persuaded out of an intense depression by the Press because: 'I am so embarrassed that I kept my cap on when my country's National Anthem was being played. I just didn't realise it was on my head.' When we told him that nobody who saw him on the rostrum—his hand in salute across his heart and tears in his eyes—could believe that he meant any disrespect, he said: 'But the colonel of my detachment will. I will just have to apologise to the American people.' What a truly incredible Olympics these are.

David Hemery, I am convinced, ran as well as he did in Mexico four years ago. Today he started in the same way—flat-out in this event that has always been known as 'man killer'. He was quickly gaining on those outside him, including Ralph Mann, the 23-year-old Californian who was one of his main rivals, and for a moment I thought that David was going to win a second gold medal. But when he changed down at the sixth flight from 13 strides to 15 strides between the hurdles, Akii-Bua changed from 13 to 14 which means that he was leading with alternate legs. That is exactly the technique which Hemery tried to learn this summer, knowing how important it would be to save four strides. Unfortunately he failed to master it.

Over the last hurdle of the second bend Hemery and Akii-Bua were together, but from that moment the tall Ugandan policeman pulled away to win in a new world record of 47·8 sec—and it is only four years since David Hemery became the first man to break 49 seconds for this tough event! In the last stride Hemery was caught by Ralph Mann and lost the silver by one hundredth of a second—48·51 seconds for Mann, 48·52 seconds for Hemery. 'I am glad that my medal and my world record have gone in this way,' said Hemery afterwards. 'I'd have hated it to have gone in a slow time.' But of course his Mexico medal has not gone. It will be with him for all time, a memento of what is still one of the classic races in Olympic history.

Both Hemery and Mann were full of wonder at the strength and potential of Akii-Bua, who is coached by a shy 32-year-old Englishman, Malcolm Arnold. Arnold comes from Northwich, Cheshire, but since 1968 he has been the chief national coach in Uganda. As Mann put it: 'It's crazy. I have done everything known to man—weight-lifting, running, hurdling—the ultimate in preparation but it is of no use at all against such talent.'

And David, of course, has done the same, taking a year's absence from his job of teaching at Millfield School and going back to Boston, Massachusetts, to prepare under coach Billy Smith—just as he did in 1968. But the question now is why did David Hemery go back on his tracks and repeat himself. Is it not enough for a man to win one Olympic gold medal and to smash the world record while doing so as David did in Mexico four years ago? Well, one of the reasons why he wanted to attempt to win another medal here in Munich was because he wanted to justify what Lillian Board wanted to do. In his own words: 'Her whole being and existence was aimed towards getting a gold medal.'

It may sound romantic—perhaps it is—but it is a thought that came into the mind of a thoroughly good man when he was wrestling with himself, knowing full well what he was going to subject himself to if he decided to go on and attempt to win the ultimate athletic prize once again. There is, you see, a simple faith in this simple, natural sport of running—that you get out of it what you put into it. It is a faith that some people have about life and it would perhaps be a true faith if life was not often so unfair, so topsy-turvy, in its values and rewards.

Before we examine his motives for going on, it may be well to reflect on one image which tells you more about the discipline which an athlete has to subject himself to than anything else. There is in Boston, at Harvard University where Dave spent last winter, an incredible air-tight bubble over an indoor wooden track. Inside, in the warm air, athletes would be prancing about in shorts and singlets going through their training routines. Outside, in a temperature well below freezing—at least 12 degrees of frost—was a muffled, track-suited David Hemery bounding through the deep snow, building his strength physically and mentally. Occasionally he would stop at the plexiglass window of the dome and peer inside, into the warmth.

He knows that it is a funny, peculiar image, but he also knows, and so does his coach, Billy Smith, that it is right for him: 'Because the hardest way for me is the best way.' It is an approach that is the very essence of the Olympics.

It is a fact that there is very little physical difference between the competitors in any Olympic final—each one of them is capable of winning but the one that does win is the one who is best prepared physically and mentally. So Hemery, before the Mexico Olympic final, reflected on the words of his coach Billy Smith: 'There are a thousand hills and sand dunes behind you and there isn't time for the others to catch up.' Thus he knew that he was the strongest man in the field and that knowledge gave him the confidence to strike for the tape as he came out of his blocks, instead of waiting until the finishing straight. In other words, he won that race four years ago before he ever went to the start. That is why he has repeated the process this year: the winter in Boston under Billy Smith, the summer in England under Fred Housden, who may be 80 years old but who is still one of the greatest hurdles coaches in the world. But first Dave had to reason with himself—to rationalise why he wanted to try again when he had already won a gold medal and broken the world record. 'Some of the reasons', he says, 'may sound fairly corny and others are basic but I had to rationalise it for myself.'

After the last Olympics he made a visit to the Paraplegic Games and this greatly affected him: 'They seem so enthusiastic and full of life. They would give anything to be in my position, to have my limbs and be able to run freely and happily. And to be someone with that talent or ability and to say "Well, I could have got to the Olympic final but I don't think I will bother" is opting out on potential.' And this feeling was reinforced by the death of Lillian Board: 'I felt an obligation there too, in that her whole being and existence was aimed at getting a gold in Munich and it was taken away from her. I joined the British team at the same time as her, in 1966, and had been friends with her and she was such a very natural, nice girl and I just felt some sort of empathy of wanting to justify what she wanted to do. That may sound a bit strange but it is a sort of parallel with the paraplegics—of someone having something taken away from them. In her case it was life and strength. I still had life and strength and I had the choice of using it or neglecting it.'

It was impossible for a man of David Hemery's character to neglect it and so last year he took his leave of absence from Millfield and went over to Boston. His simple life there consisted of two training sessions every day around the snow-covered roads, up the sand dunes, over the hills, reaching a peak of 22 miles in one day. That is a very, very tough schedule for a man whose event lasts less than fifty seconds. 'Of course it got to me mentally,' he says. 'I was fed up many times, times when I thought "What am I doing this for?"' But Billy Smith kept him at it saying: 'It is going in and it can come out later on.'

But while David was going through his training programme in Boston, John Akii-Bua was at home in Uganda: 'Where it rains most of the time but when I was able to run I would wear a 25 lb jacket and run for 1500 metres over 3 foot 3 inch hurdles.' That is a training schedule that really does make the mind boggle.

And his family statistics are mind boggling. As he put it: 'I am one of forty-three families. My father was a sportsman.' This transpired to mean that he was one of 43 children, his father having had eight wives and also being interested in shooting! And then he went through the athletic potential of the Akii-Bua clan: three younger brothers who are already 6 feet 2 inches high jumpers and two 12-year-old boys (they could be twins or sons of different wives—it is hard to tell) who can triple jump 44 feet, which is good for a boy five years older. John himself says that he is going home to get married so there will, no doubt, be more Akii-Buas at the Olympics in the year 2000.

Perhaps because he is on his honeymoon, Dave Wottle seemed

disinterested in the heats and semi-finals of the 800 metres—he just waits for all the others to do the work and then slips through in the finishing straight. But I thought he had misjudged the final of the 800 metres today and so did he: 'All the way', he said afterwards, 'I was just running to catch up.'

He was twenty yards down on the leaders after 300 metres and this is a bit much. At the bell he had closed to the back of the field but he was still well out of the race on the final bend. But Arzhanov of Russia, who looks like a darker version of Rudolf Nureyev, had made his effort too early, taking the lead from Mike Boit and Robert Ouko of Kenya as they flagged on the back straight. Yet Arzhanov is a man who can always accelerate twice and he did so as he hit the finishing straight. By now Wottle had improved to fourth, his ridiculous dirty white golf cap making him look like a flying duck. 'I was ready to concede the race', he said afterwards, 'but then Boit flagged and I thought I had the silver. Then I saw Arzhanov letting off and I thought I might get him.' He did, exactly one stride before the line, with Arzhanov throwing himself across the finish in desperation.

In a chaotic Press conference afterwards with American and Russian journalists almost smothering the two athletes, one might have thought one was listening to two complete failures. Arzhanov was staring bleakly at his hands almost on the verge of tears and Wottle, his hat removed at last, was utterly disconsolate at what he regarded as his insult to the American flag. He is an army boy from Ohio in the Mid-West and they take such things very seriously there.

And so to the British performances: A courageous one from Andy Carter who came sixth in the 800 metres with the very respectable time of 1 min 46·6 sec (Dave Wottle's winning time was 1 min 45·9 sec, a long way off the world record which he shares with Ralph Doubell at 1 min 44·3 sec); and a most amazing performance from big Mary Peters. She is 33 years old, 5 feet 8 inches tall and weighs 11 stone, single and charming and today, after three events in the five-event pentathlon, she leads by 97 points with a total of 2969—a points score which nobody else has ever achieved on the first day of a pentathlon. Behind her with 2872 points is the world record holder Burglinde Pollak of East Germany and Heide Rosendahl, the darling of the German crowd and the European champion, is in fifth place with 2668. But tomorrow Mary has her two weakest events: the long jump and the 200 metres which happen to be

Fraulein Rosendahl's strongest events—she is, after all the Olympic champion in the long jump.

But experts who have worked out this complex event believe that Mary after performing wondrously today, has a commanding lead. So if David Bedford does not win a gold medal in the 10,000 metres tomorrow (and, quite frankly, nobody whose judgement I respect believes that he will do so) then Mary might well save our British honour. Perhaps she was inspired today by a monumental row with some German officials. Early this morning, before anyone's normal breakfast time, Mary and Ann Wilson went to warm up in the indoor stadium because it was raining. Their way was barred until the British women's team manager, Marea Hartman, kicked up such a fuss that the officials let her in. There inside was Heide Rosendahl, warming up in peace and keeping dry from the rain!

When the competition proper started Mary ran 13·29 sec in the 100 metres hurdles, put the shot 53 feet 1¼ inches (only 5 inches below her British record) and then high jumped 5 feet 10½ inches—a personal best. It is a peaceful change for her, being in the Olympic village. The day she left Belfast there were three explosions within 300 yards of her flat.

Forgive me if I am a little parochial and record some rather mediocre performances—by Olympic standards—by some of the British girls, but one of those involved was Janet Simpson and I can remember meeting someone in my local pub who said that he had followed Janet Simpson's career for many years now and that her performances on the track had always given him great delight. 'She never seems to get the credit she deserves,' he said, 'and many is the time that I've found myself almost crying for her.' So for that unknown admirer of Janet Simpson let me unhappily recall that she spent a very unhappy 27th birthday today and was eliminated in the 400 metres heats in the slow time of 54·13 sec. Andrea Lynch, the 19-year-old London bank clerk, was outclassed in the semi-finals of the 100 metres—the gold medal being won eventually by the powerful East German girl, Renate Stecher, who is as superior to her rivals in the women's sprint as Valeri Borzov was to his rivals in the men's sprint.

Except for Dave Wottle's very unexpected win in the 800 metres this has been a wretched games for American athletes so far. Today they lost the pole vault for the first time since 1896. It was an East

Olga Korbut, the 17-year-old from Russia who captured three gold medals and everybody's hearts.

Mary Peters on the victory rostrum.
Left: SUPERCALIFRAGILISTICEXPIALIDOSO with Rodney Pattisson and Chris Davies as crew. This was Rodney Pattisson's second gold medal.

Above: Spitz waives the rules of amateurism as he salutes.

Below left: Shane Gould; she won three gold medals in the water and always carried her kangaroo mascot out of the water.

Below right: David Wilkie from Edinburgh, who won a silver medal in the 200 metres breaststroke.

3

4 *Above left and right:* The victor and the vanquished. Frank Shorter (U.S.A.) the winner of the Marathon and Ron Hill who came sixth.
Not until a third of the distance had been covered in the 3000 metres steeplechase final did the real steeplechasers start to test Kip Keino. Here Bron Malinowski of Poland (729) sets the pace out of the water jump. Behind him (*right to left*) are Dousan Moravcik of Czechoslovakia (879), Ben Jipcho of Kenya (574) with the 1968 gold medallist Amos Biwott behind him, Kip Keino (576) and Tapio Kantanen (207) of Finland. The final order was Keino, Jipcho, Kantanen.

Above left: On the first day of the track and field programme, an athlete from the host country won the first field event gold medal. Heide Rosendahl winning the long jump with a leap of 22 ft 3 in.

Above right: Bob Seagren (U.S.A.) the defending champion in the pole vault, did not like the pole which he was allocated. After coming second (the first time that the United States have ever failed to win this event) he handed the pole back angrily.

Below left: Lynn Davies, Olympic and Commonwealth Games gold medallist and European champion, but now at the age of 30 unable to qualify for the final. His best jump of 25 ft 0¾ in was two feet below his best. A sad end to a great career.

Below right: Alan Lerwill trying to jump through the glass roof of the stadium.

6 Mix up in the heats of the 1500 metres—and nobody knows what really happened. Jim Ryun (U.S.A.) the world record holder falls after being tripped up by—or tripping—Billy Fordjour (Ghana) who is concealed behind No. 912, Vitus Ashaba (Uganda). Ryun got up and completed the race but afterwards he could give no explanation of what really happened.

Above: Dave Wottle—*the Head Waiter*. Wottle said that he was always trying to catch up and he did do so right on the line to win the 800 metres.
Below: Six days after suffering the misery of defeat in the individual 400 metres, David Jenkins celebrates a silver medal in the 4 × 400 metres relay.

7

Above left: Valeri Borzov of Russia, the first man to win the sprint double since Bobby Morrow of the United States in 1956.

Above right: The most outstanding woman athlete of the games—Russia's Ludmilla Bragina who broke the world record three times at Munich for the 1500 metres.

Below left: Lasse Viren looking comfortable and confident on the way to his first gold medal in the 10,000 metres final.

Below right: The powerful Renate Stecher (147) of East Germany completes the sprint double, by winning the 200 metres. Raelene Boyle (Australia) was second.

Above: One of the sensations of the Games, Ulrike Meyfarth, only just 16, won the High Jump with a world record equalling jump of 6 ft 3½ in.

Below left: The strongest woman in the world; Nadizhda Chizhova (U.S.S.R.) winning the shot put with a new world record.

Below right: George Woods (U.S.A.) who came second in the men's shot put.

10 'How many more laps to go . . .?' 'Don't ask me, mate.' *Above left:* Dave Bedford (274) and Emile Puttemans (61) comfortably chatting as they beat the Olympic record in a heat of the 10,000 metres.

Above right: The crucial moment in the 1500 metres. Pekka Vasala of Finland (226) passes Kip Keino.

Below: The moment we knew that David Hemery (288) had lost his 400 metres hurdles title. John Akii-Bua (Uganda) in the inside lane lands first as they come into the finishing straight.

Above: Olga Korbut.
Below: Ludmila Tourischeva, the 19-year-old Olympic champion in the combined exercises.

Above: Princess Anne, European Three Day Event Champion in 1971 had to withdraw from the list of Olympic possibles when her horse Doublet was injured. A very happy spectator in Munich, as she watches Richard Meade win the individual gold medal.

Below: The victorious Three Day Event team. (*from left to right*) Mark Phillips, Mary Gordon-Watson, Richard Meade and Bridget Parker.

Above: Richard Meade takes one of the jumps during his individual gold medal winning round on Laurieston.

Below: In trying to beat Grazino Mancinelli's time in the jump off for the individual medal, Ann Moore took a corner too fast and the gallant Psalm refused—and that cost her three faults and the gold medal.

Above: One of the oddest of many odd decisions in the Boxing Hall was Dieter Kottysch's (West Germany) 'win' over Alan Minter (G.B.) in the semi-finals of the light middleweight division.

Below: Ralph Evans from Waterlooville in Hampshire looks in command but he lost this semi-final to Gedo of Hungary.

Above: Outstanding gold medal winner Teofilo Stevenson's left hand lands on the chin of the white American hope Duane Bobick.

Below left: Vassili Alexeyev, 23 st 4 lb, who won the super heavyweight title with a total weight of 1411 pounds.

Below right: The small British Judo team were phenomenally successful. Dave Starbrook (*top*) won a silver medal in the light heavyweight class, and Brian Jacks won a bronze medal in the middleweight class.

16 *Above:* The supple Spaniard: Fernandez Ochoa, who won the slalom at Sapporo.

Right: Janet Lynn in Sapporo; 'there was a movement when she moved backwards so that her blonde hair flew forwards and her arms were outstretched and she was indeed the embodiment of a young girl in love with the world.'

German, Wolfgang Nordwig, who beat the reigning champion, Bob Seagren with a vault of 18 ft 0½ inch. It is really Seagren and not Wottle who should be censored for his behaviour today. He refused to shake hands with Nordwig after the event and ceremoniously handed his pole to Adrian Paulen, the Dutchman who runs the technical side of world athletics. It was supposed to be a sign of disgust, because Seagren had not been allowed to use his own special pole which has just been developed in the United States and which is supposed to be better than any other sort of pole. But the Olympics are about who is the best athlete not about who has the best equipment.

While all this was going on in the stadium, a British swimmer was at last achieving a worthy result in the swimming pool, no more than 200 yards away. Up to now the British swimming team have really done appallingly badly. None of them can explain, not even the team manager, John Verrier, how it is that most of them have consistently failed in the racing pool to get anywhere near the times they have been recording in training. But today David Wilkie, an 18-year-old Edinburgh student, produced a brilliant performance in the 200 metres breast stroke. At the halfway mark he was only in sixth position but while the others began to fade he turned on the power and forged steadily through the field. He did not catch the American world record holder, John Hencken, who was, frankly, in a class of his own, but he did catch the Japanese, Taguchi, to win the silver medal by a touch.

David folds his long hair into a white bathing cap, which seems to me a lot more sensible than shaving your head as one of the German swimmers did earlier in the week—apparently in an effort to get smoother progress through the water. It did win the German a bronze medal and when he went on to the victory stand he put on a long blond wig. Some people take their sport to ridiculous lengths.

Today has also been finals day in the rowing course but so much takes place at these Games that I have not had an opportunity to go out and see what has been happening there so I have asked my good friend and colleague, John Rodda, the rowing correspondent of *The Guardian*, to write about the rowing events.

8
'AN ELATED FEELING WHICH HELPED NUMB THE PAIN'

by John Rodda

Oberschleissheim, the rowing course, was a place of escape. After the clamour and claustrophobia of the Olympic city and its Press Centre, it seemed odd going to the Olympic Games down winding lanes with corn and maize leaning in the breeze on one side and young pines on the other. But there in the middle of some fields the Germans had built the last word—so they believed—in rowing courses.

With mounds and silver birches and soft brown wood they had created beauty. The buildings were massive, but unlike the main centre people were not overwhelmed by them because there was space. Driving into the area between the boathouses and the administration centre was like arriving at a large, chic motel. The stand held three thousand spectators comfortably but the greatest moment of pride for the Germans must have been in the two boathouse doors which remained shut, unneeded. Here they were accommodating the world's greatest collection of oarsmen in the finest facilities, and there were two boathouse sections to spare. But when you spend £8 million on a course then you can afford to over-estimate a little.

But if there were moments of pride for the Germans there were some of humiliation. They have a great rowing tradition and to take only one gold medal and one bronze was a disappointment. But the greater blow came three days before the finals when Thomas Keller, the Swiss millionaire who is president of the International Rowing

Federation (F.I.S.A.), went on the public address system and said in French, German and English (he is capable of another four languages) that the conditions were unfair.

In shelling out £8 million on the course the Germans had gone to great lengths to ensure that whatever the wind strength and direction the conditions for rowing in each lane would be similar. The Germans were so convinced they had got this aspect correct that they said so each day in the programme notes. Yet here was Keller saying that they were wrong and that racing would be delayed until there was an improvement. The wind was blowing at between 10 and 14 miles an hour at a slight angle to the length of the course and the difference between lanes one and two, and lanes five and six was nearly 2 m.p.h.; in fact the television pictures from the starting area showed that there were, occasionally, white horses.

After an hour and twenty minutes Keller allowed racing to start, but in fact the conditions were really no better. Water was breaking over the saxboards and keeping the boats straight at the start was extremely difficult. Before the semi-finals were over the arithmetic showed that lanes 5 and 6 could justifiably be named 'Losersstrasse'. The only crews from these lanes to finish first or second, in their semi-final, also went on to win gold or silver medals.

At the end of the day Keller admitted the unfairness and pointed particularly to the lightweight crews and specifically three British ones—the coxless four, the single scull and the coxed pair—who might have got to the final in different circumstances.

By the day of the finals the wind had abated and the competition was undoubtedly the finest of any Olympic regatta. While the East Germans won a medal in every one of the seven events—three of them gold—the tightness of the competition indicates that other systems are not far off the prizes. The most stirring moment was in the blue riband event of the regatta, the eights final, when all the sophisticated expertise of the Europeans and the deep tradition of the Americans was swept aside by a bunch of lean Kiwis who blasted their way to victory without compromise. They had been to Europe twelve months before and won at Copenhagen in the European championships, but a non-rowing nation does not pull that sort of stroke twice.

The New Zealanders had it hard in more aspects than on the water. Rowing does not command great support back home and to live and work together for the eleven weeks which their coach, Rusty Robinson, believed was necessary cost a lot of money and they also had to persuade the public to subscribe, through raffles and other money-spinning methods, towards their Olympic costs. It amounted to something like £21,000 which is a lot of money to be thinking about when you are training for the greatest sporting moment of your life.

Robinson, with plenty of tall men in the boat, used their natural assets, which was to dig the blade deep to ensure maximum propulsion. To make them even more effective he opted for a style which is the antithesis of rowing tradition. The body was kept much closer to upright at the beginning of the stroke and stayed like that instead of the more traditional long lean back. The effect looks awkward and rigid and unnatural, and so it would be unless the body was conditioned to take this kind of strain. Which is what Robinson and his men had been working on for a year. That lean forward and back bending movement, which takes so much energy, was eliminated and the power thus saved was transferred to the first objective, driving the blade through the water. To rowing men this may seem infuriatingly simple but this is basically how New Zealand covered the 2000 metres faster than anyone else.

Tactically too they were very brave. They went off at 45 strokes to the minute, all hard, deep pulls on the blade, and over the first half the course they never let the rating go below 38½, while the Americans, the Russians and the East Germans had slid down to 37 and 36. At the halfway point the men in black were a length and a little bit of daylight ahead of the nearest crew, the Russians. It was an elated feeling which helped numb the pain. A lot of other people had to do a lot of work to dislodge them; the Americans, the West and East Germans tried in the third 500 metres and the East Germans managed to get an overlap—in fact the New Zealand lead at one point was down to no more than two-thirds of a length. But that is as close as anyone came.

However, this was not the full extent of New Zealand power and, but for the greatest quartet in rowing history, the Kiwis would have taken a second gold. The most famous names in rowing are Frank Forberger, Frank Ruehle, Dieter Grahn and Dieter Schubert. They come from the Einhert Club in Dresden and they first won a world title in coxless fours in 1966. Since that time they have been unbeaten in major events, winning two Olympic gold medals, another world title and two European titles. The incentives to go on rowing in East Germany are, perhaps, greater than in most other places, but to maintain the level they have achieved over a period of six years, particularly as it involves four people, is phenomenal in any sport.

The New Zealand four got within one and a half seconds—in nearly 6½ minutes rowing—of dislodging them in a manner that was just as exciting as the rowing of their eight. The two crews, in adjacent lanes just to make it more spectacular, pulled away together at the 500 metres mark, where the electronic timing had the Germans ahead by 21 hundredths of a second. In the next 500 metres the position was almost the same, except that the New Zealand bow was pushing ahead first as each stroke was made. But here they attacked, raising their rating yet holding the quality of their work and driving in a wedge. With 500 metres left the East Germans were nearly a boat length down but in that final stretch of water came the most tantalising, most highly pitched moments of the regatta.

The Germans hardened their stroke and hit a rating that inexorably gnawed at New Zealand's lead. There was no panic on either station, no flurry to up the rating, for each four was stretched to its limit. The New Zealanders hoping and hanging on; the Germans feeling at every marker buoy that the pendulum—a gold one—was swinging their way. Not until the last five strokes did they get a lead and New Zealand knew that their finely based judgement, to bring down the world's toughest crew, had been only slightly miscalculated. The fractions on the watches are human misjudgements magnified to enormity in the difference between gold and silver.

One of the first men to arrive in the Olympic Village was Alberto Demiddi, an Argentinian with a mop of rich brown hair, bronzed and powerful arms. His singing and the large posters draped around the walls and windows puzzled the Germans but it was all part of the Demiddi method of building confidence. His power in sculling had been demonstrated in most places, including Henley, where a South American commentator extolled his virtues down a telephone line to Buenos Aires for 2½ hours—all for eight minutes' sculling—and in the European championships in Copenhagen. Demiddi has the ability to scull opponents down by rowing for a long stretch at something below a sprint. He has the power and the precision to keep going and finally destroy those scullers who try bursts to get them into a position from where they can sit in front. It worked in his heat and semi-final but in the final he found himself alongside Yuri Malishev of Russia, the other favourite for the title. Malishev broke into the top echelon of sculling during the summer and scored a startlingly easy win at Lucerne.

Malishev led off from the start which was really no worry to the Demiddi fans. The Argentinian's rhythm was excellent and Malishev never had more than two-thirds of a length in hand. By 1000 metres the position was the same and somewhere in the next 500 metres that long pull, at 31 strokes to the minute, would devour the Russian. But it did not. At 1500 metres the gap between the pair was 1½ seconds and Malishev was sculling without hint of being broken. By 1750 metres Demiddi was still making no impression and for the first time in four years he had a challenge he could not match—he was unable to get those bronzed, rippling, muscled arms to produce a sprint, a quick rise in strike which might have nipped the Russian's lead. Demiddi went on steadily and methodically, but unable to shift the man in the red shirt from first place.

The British part in all these events, judged by the rising hopes of June and July, was disappointing, but judged by events of the previous October it was a success. British rowing had reached a new low in September 1971 at the European championships and as a result the international future was placed in the hands of Bob Janousek, the chief national coach and a Czech. He produced a scheme which detached the top forty oarsmen from their clubs and domestic competition.

They worked in groups around the country, training far more intensively than ever before. That sort of plan does not produce Olympic winners in ten months, though by June our double scull, Pat Delafield and Tim Crooks, was going so well that they were being mentioned as medallists; and then suddenly a new coxed pair David Maxwell and Mike Hart, who were in the Cambridge eight earlier in the year, emerged as a possibility. There was of course the enigmatic Ken Dwan, who reached the Mexico final but had shown no outstanding form since; and the Thames Tradesmen four, a weedy quartet who worked as hard as anyone and were beginning to get rewards. In the event only one crew reached a final, the double scull, and they, after leading for most of the first half of the race, faded. They were wrongly rigged for the sudden change in the strength of the wind.

Having got every crew to the semi-final stage (something the British had never before achieved in an Olympic Games) what then followed was something of an anti-climax. But if this sort of change could be produced in ten months with a fair amount of makeshift methods, then what can be achieved in another four years?

9
'OR WHAT'S A HEAVEN FOR?'

Sunday, September 3rd

Where do we start? With victory or defeat? At the risk of being accused that journalists always concentrate on the bad news I am going to start with defeat, for in that defeat lies so much of the human spirit, the spirit which Robert Browning captured so perfectly in those two lines:

> Ah, but a man's reach should escape his grasp,
> Or what's a heaven for?

Dave Bedford, an immature boy of 22, reached for a gold medal today and was totally unable to grasp it. I do not believe there was anything wrong with him physically, but mentally this boy was up against a lot of strong-willed men and it was the men who triumphed. Dave did what everybody had expected—he went to the front and hammered out a hard pace—60·6 sec for the first lap which is fast enough for a miler. But they all stayed with him. After four laps—not yet a sixth of the distance—that tough little man from Ethiopia, Merus Yifter, came up to Dave's shoulder as if to say, 'you can't worry us with this pace'. But on went Bedford hammering out the strides and I use the word 'hammer' with intent because there was nothing fluid, nothing relaxed about his running today.

After five laps Dave was 6·2 sec inside Ron Clarke's world record time. At 3000 metres he was leading the field with a time of 8 min 0·4 sec which would have been a world record for that distance until

Gordon Pirie broke it in the mid 1950s. But then, after eight laps Yifter played his mental game once again, going up to Bedford's shoulder, and, briefly, taking the lead as if to say 'the pace is not fast enough'. And so they ran with Dave surging down every back straight and those who knew what it was all about let him go, knowing that they would catch him again as he slowed on the bottom bend. At the half way mark (12½ laps run and 12½ laps still to go) Dave slowed so suddenly that there was a pile up behind him—Frank Shorter tripped Lasse Viren who stumbled on to his hands and Gammoudi fell over Viren's body and lay spreadeagled on the track. Viren was up quickly and chased the field. Perhaps Dave was unaware of what had happened because the pace slowed rather than quickened and Viren was with the leading bunch within a lap. In another couple of laps this slight and lightly bearded Finnish policeman was in the lead and Bedford's challenge was over.

And so they ran, with Viren stretching their bodies and crucifying their hearts. With seven laps to go Dave had fallen back to eighth position but that was as far as he would allow himself to go. Now the race was between Viren, Yifter of Ethiopia, Shorter of the United States, Haro of Spain and Puttemans of Belgium. Bedford tried to catch them but that is an impossible task once contact has been broken.

At the bell Viren was in the lead and only Puttemans was in touch. Down the back straight they flew and as they entered the final bend Puttemans glanced over his shoulder and I knew that his mind had settled for a silver medal. And so it was: Viren coming home comfortably in a new world record of 27 min 38·4 sec with Puttemans second and Yifter third. Dave was sixth a very long way—some 70 yards—behind Frank Shorter who was fifth.

Dave walked straight to the tunnel leading to the dressing rooms without congratulating Viren and put his hand over the lens of the official film camera. It was an ungracious act but it is not easy for a young man to be gracious when his dream has been shattered. The Press were waiting for him and he said: 'Give me ten minutes' as he went into the dressing room. Three-quarters of an hour later he emerged, towel over his head to hide his tears and ran back to the Olympic Village like, as Peter Wilson put it, 'a wounded animal seeking to hide'. It is his pride, his confidence, that has been mortally wounded.

What now? Can a man ever recover from such a thrashing, from such a collapse of all his hopes. The answer to that must surely be 'yes'. The clue lies perhaps in something that Dave himself said: 'Sometimes people don't remember that I am only 22.' Remember how Mary Bignal 'failed' in Rome in 1960 and came back to win in 1964? Remember how Mark Spitz 'failed' in Mexico and came back to win four individual gold medals in 1972? One searing experience in an athlete's life can only do him good, can only strengthen his resolve that he is indeed going to win that on which he has set his heart. But, of course, there must be doubt because this is not Dave's first such traumatic experience. Remember his confidence before the European championships in Helsinki in 1971, a confidence that was shattered by another Finn, Juha Vaatainen? Please do not ask me whether I believe that Bedford will rehabilitate himself because I cannot—nor can anyone—see into his mind. People react so differently in adversity: some become stronger, more resilient; some are defeated with utter finality. I have said it before but I will say it again: I do believe that Bedford could rehabilitate himself, could become the greatest distance runner the world has ever seen if only he could find someone of experience and maturity, someone who knows all the modern techniques of training, with whom he could share the burden of a modern athlete's life.

Perhaps he, and indeed the whole athletic fraternity in Britain, could learn from what has been happening in Finland these last few years. Between the wars Finland was the greatest athletic nation in the world—indeed Finland with a population of only four and a half million people (less than the population of Scotland) could have taken on the rest of the world in the middle and long distance events and beaten them. In the five Olympic Games held between the wars Finland won thirty out of a possible total of sixty medals in four events—1500 metres, 5000 metres, 10,000 metres and 3000 metres steeplechase. Indeed, on one occasion, the 10,000 metres in the 1936 Games, Finnish athletes came first, second and third. But since the war Finnish athletes have not won one single medal of any sort in these events—until today. Do not think that they have found just one great athlete—Lasse Viren. They also have Juha Vaatainen who, because of a knee injury, could not run today, but who will run in the 5000 metres this coming week; and also Pekka Vasala who is the favourite for the 1500 metres; and Kantanen who runs in the

3000 metres steeplechase tomorrow with a great chance of a medal.

I always believed that the demise of Finnish athletics after the war was due simply to the statistical facts of life—that a nation of less than five million people could not compete against all the teeming millions who have now achieved a sufficient standard of living to free them to take part in sport. But the Finns believed it was because of their winter. Before the war it was sufficient if an athlete started to train in the spring, but by 1952 it was absolutely necessary to put in a solid base of stamina work throughout the winter and, so the Finns said, you can't do that when the temperature is 30° below freezing and the snow is feet deep. But, of course, the lack of success, the collapse of their tradition, worried them. Had they lost their 'sisu', that very special Finnish quality which the Russians discovered to their cost when they invaded Finland? Loosely translated it means 'fighting guts' and it comes from every fibre of their body and minds. There is certainly no greater insult to a Finn than to say he has no 'sisu'.

So they did something about it. They imported Arthur Lydiard from New Zealand—the man who coached Peter Snell and Murray Halberg and many other good New Zealand athletes. He is a little man, tough, bubbling with energy, an extrovert and a great coach. He has the same qualities as Gerschler of Germany, Igloi of Hungary (now in America), Stampfl of Austria (and also of Britain and now in Australia), and our own Geoff Dyson, who was so contained by the system in Britain that he had to escape to Canada.

Lydiard did not have an easy time in Finland. Their Press wanted instant success, yet he knew that it would take three to five years. But the coaches listened to him and so did the athletes when they saw him going out training when the temperature was 30° below zero. And there was an administrator and planner, Jukka Uunila, President of the Finnish Olympic Committee, who believed in him and backed him. Lydiard thought that the Finns had become too artificial in their training, doing it all on the tracks of which there is a plentiful supply—ten tracks, for instance, in Tampere where Lydiard lived, a town of 160,000 people. He put them back on to the road in the depths of winter and into their beautiful forests as soon as the weather allowed. When he left at the end of his contract after two years, he had helped to set up a new system—one product of which is Lasse Viren, the man who broke Bedford.

Viren is an 'A' class athlete—the top class naturally—which

means that he has something over £1000 put at his disposal, or rather at the disposal of his coach. No cash is given to him because that would infringe the amateur laws, but bills for food and equipment and travelling expenses are paid. And the same is true of all the other top class Finnish athletes.

'You think', said a Finnish journalist to me, 'that the big days are here again for Finnish track. No, the biggest days are not here yet. It is still too early.'

If only we had such a system in Britain, but of course we will not while we retain our present system of amateur officials who are too jealous of their power to ever hand it over to professionals.

But let us turn to a happier subject—big, blonde, bubbling, Mary Peters. She has captured the heart not only of the British supporters, who had already given her their hearts, but of the whole packed stadium here in Munich. Last night they stayed in their thousands to will her over the high jump, chanting her name like a soccer crowd chants the name of its favourite team. But today it was tough for Mary. In the long jump that favourite of all Western Germany, Heide Rosendahl—Heide of the spectacles and the long red and white ringed socks—leapt 22 feet 5 inches, further than she jumped when she won the long jump gold medal in the stadium on Thursday. And Mary could only manage 19 feet 7½ inches.

So at lunch time when there was one more event to go (the 200 metres) the experts got to work with their tables and calculated that if Heide achieved her personal best of 23·1 seconds then Mary also had to run as fast as she had ever done—24·2 seconds—if she was to win the gold medal. They were drawn in the same heat and I focused my binoculars on to these two big girls. They were both out of their blocks and running hard and for a second it seemed to me that Mary might even be holding the German girl around the bend but it was an optical illusion.

As they came into the straight Heide was a good three yards clear and Mary, who is really too large to be a good sprinter, was struggling in her wake. But she struggled to mighty effect. The German girl went past the finishing post in 22·9 sec—her best ever. And now we had to wait for Mary's time. And so did she—an agonising few minutes. Then the electronic flashboard stuttered . . . 24 . . . 08. Mary had won by a mere 10 points. Never has a nicer girl—I should say a nicer woman for she is 33 years old—won a gold medal. Afterwards while I was interviewing her in the television studio in the bowels of the stadium, the door opened while we were on the air, and her father Arthur, whom Mary had not seen for two years, walked into the studio. It was an emotional, very private moment, that everybody in Britain saw on their television screens.

Ten miles away another blonde British girl was winning a silver medal. Ann Moore is 21 years old and very pretty. She—and her horse Psalm, the youngest rider and the smallest horse in the field of fifty-six who contested the Olympic Grand Prix—was one of only three to qualify for the jump off.

Neal Shapiro of America on Sloopy was the first to jump and he had eight faults in 46 seconds. Then went the experienced Italian, Graziano Mancinelli, on Ambassador and he was clear with the time of 45 seconds. Ann knew that she had to ride Psalm very hard indeed if she was to beat this time and ride him hard she did. They were clear over the first fence and then she turned Psalm fast heading for the second at an acute angle. Her eyes and mind were concentrated on it but Psalm was looking straight ahead at the crowd and it was only in the last two or three strides that this mighty second fence came into his view. It was just too much for him and he refused. Given a second chance and he leapt it with a foot to spare but that refusal cost them three points and the gold medal.

As Ann said later: 'I had either to go for a safe silver or try for the gold against the clock and I just took that second fence too sharply.' But how much better it is to attempt the supreme prize rather than settle for second best.

It is very easy for other members of the Olympic team who have got to Munich through sweat and fatigue and searing lungs, to be patronising, indeed envious, of these show jumpers who appear to have an animal to do all the work and doubly envious of someone like Ann Moore, who seems to have every advantage in life. She is the eldest of six children of a very well off Midlands industrialist who also happens to have a good eye for a horse.

It was her father, Norman, who bought Psalm as a four-year-old from a Derbyshire farmer—originally as a hunter for Ann who was then only 15 years old. But he was so obviously talented as a jumper that Ann converted him to show jumping and on him she won the European Ladies' Championship in Switzerland last year. He is very well bred, being by a sprinter sire, Sermon, out of a mare by the

Derby winner Pinza. Ann has a great affection for him: 'He's a champion. Some of them are born champions and Psalm is a champion. He has a great egotistical attitude—"everyone look at me because I'm terribly good".

'He was difficult as a young horse and his attitude of "don't you tell me what to do", is rather like people who are difficult. If you can channel them the right way that devilment becomes sheer brilliance—if it runs the other way it can be disastrous so he has to be watched. He's very difficult in the stable. It's his domain and you are not particularly welcome in there unless you're there to feed him. That's him. Psalm is a champion.'

In a way that is also a very good description, I believe, of Ann herself, although, of course, it does not fit exactly. Any really top class sportsman has to be egotistical, has to look after himself first, has to be increasingly selfish. She is aware of the danger. 'Everyone' —she is talking about those at the top—'is a little bit of an island. I think you have to be really. I know I have become more selfish already. But then I have to look at it another way. I wonder how many other people are able to do exactly what they want to do and be happy doing it and live a life that completely suits them. I'm very, very fortunate to have landed in a slot that suits me.'

She seems to have no fear, certainly not of horses or of jumps however big, despite the fact that she is scarred all over and has cracked her skull, broken her jaw, one leg, both collar bones, some ribs and suffered various other dislocations. And she is competitive, despite that old cliché, so often true, that there must be some desperate need to succeed. Yet she has never really wanted for any material thing in her life. 'You're right in a sense. Yes, of course, hungry fighters are the best. But there is also a sense of achievement. Either you're the type of person who wants to go and do well and make something of your life or you're not. I think that's true no matter what circumstances you are born in.'

And when she smiles at you like that you cannot, if you are a man, do anything but agree.

10
'IT SEEMS I'M JUST A BOY AMONG MEN'

Monday, September 4th

This is the day on which a 16-year-old American swimmer had his gold medal taken away from him because he took the medicine prescribed by his doctor. This is the day on which Mark Spitz won his seventh, and last gold medal; Kip Keino won his 'spare' event; and a young Edinburgh University student confessed: 'It seems I am just a boy among men.'

Today that student, David Jenkins, failed to reach the final of the 400 metres. This morning he had an easy passage in his second round heat, winning in 45·99 seconds and making it look all very easy. But this afternoon he had a very hard task, being drawn in the same semi-final as two of the Americans, Vince Matthews and John Smith, Charles Asati of Kenya and Karl Honz of West Germany. He was drawn in the outside lane, which he likes, despite the fact that he is unable to see the other runners until he hits the finishing straight. He started fast, perhaps too fast, and there was little doubt that he was leading at the halfway mark. But as soon as they came into the finishing straight his head began to jerk and his whole body tightened. Mid-way down the straight he glanced inside him and saw four men ahead and in that moment he knew that his Olympic effort was over. He was fifth in a time of 45·9 seconds—0·6 seconds slower than his own British record set earlier this year. Fifth in the semi-final when he was hoping to win the final. How does one explain such form?

David himself said: 'I just blew it. It seems I am just a boy among men.' But it is not as easy as that. There could be a physical reason: David had a heavy head cold and I respect him for never using this as an excuse. There could be a mental reason: that all his fire and energy has been left on the training track at Meadowbank in Edinburgh: that he is in fact 'stale'. 'Staleness' is a strange phenomenon that affects athletes. Physically they should be at the top of their form but somehow there is no spark left and they run well below their best. It is entirely mental and there are only two cures for it—a long rest or a complete change of training.

Both David and his coach, John Anderson, have had only one objective throughout this year: to win the 400 metres final at 5.30 p.m. tomorrow afternoon—anything else would be failure in the eyes of both these men. And now they are tasting failure. They must wonder about all those days spent on the tartan track of the Meadowbank stadium—built for the 1970 Commonwealth Games: Anderson at the end of the straight, stopwatch in hand, shouting 'harder, harder, harder'; Jenkins, every particle of his body alive with energy, striding, floating, pounding, fighting his way through a sea of lactic acid towards his coach.

When I visited them this summer it was on a day of light training because David had been out on that track three times the previous day. Yet he ran 60 metres three times, in 6·1 sec, and 6·0 sec and 6·0 sec; 100 metres twice in 9·8 and 9·9 sec; and 150 yards once in 13·6 sec. Only the last effort satisfied either of them. Of course, 9·8 sec for a 100 metres is faster than the world record from a stationary start, but David was using a flying start. All this training, and it had been going on for most of the summer, was in aid of one 100 metres—the last 100 metres of the 400 metre final on September 6th. 'For the first time in his life', said Anderson, 'David will probably not be clearly in front when he comes off the final bend. He may well have two or three other people with him and for the last 100 metres they will race shoulder to shoulder and that will be the test—the true test of the man. Has his character got what it takes to stand up to this? There will be those that will fail and those who will go on.'

And then he went on: 'If David is as great an athlete as I believe him to be physically and mentally and emotionally then I think at that stage it is possible that the David Jenkins control situation may undergo a slight reorganisation and he may find depths that even

David Jenkins didn't realise were there. Perhaps it is unfair of me to say that about a boy who is only 20, but when you get to the stage where the only targets you can aim for are the very highest then you can't start making excuses for the fact that he is only 20. You accept that this is a man. . . .'

So do we now accept that David is not a man because he failed today? The answer to that is: 'no'. It is simply that he is lacking in experience and perhaps still lacking in strength for those last vital 100 metres in the longest sprint race in the athletic calendar.

Now to Kip Keino, that courteous gentleman from Kenya. He is the reigning 1500 metres Olympic champion, having beaten Jim Ryun, the world record holder, in Mexico four years ago. And of course he is entered again in the 1500 metres here in Munich. But one Olympic event is not enough to satisfy Kip's joy in running. His other natural event is the 5000 metres and he was rather upset earlier in the year when he discovered that the athletic programme here in Munich denied him the opportunity of running the 5000 metres as it clashed with the 1500 metres. So he studied the programme and realised that he would be able to combine his speciality with the 3000 metres steeplechase. He had never run the event before this year and indeed had only run it four times before the Games opened. But today he won, with ease, and was only two seconds outside the world record!

His steeplechasing style is nothing less than appalling: he himself admits that 'I run the event like an animal'. Sometimes he hurdles the barriers and sometimes he puts his foot on the top, but he is such a great runner on the flat that it does not seem to make much difference. However, the true steeplechasers played into his hands by setting off at a dawdle. If they wanted to beat Keino they ought to have stretched out from the start of the race so that his indifferent technique would have taken its toll of his strength. But instead they ambled through the first 1000 metres in 2 min 54·4 sec and hardly increased the pace for the next 1000 metres which took 2 min 49·1 sec. It was at this point that Kip moved up to join his team mates, Amos Biwott (the steeplechase champion in Mexico) and Ben Jipcho. With three Kenyans in the first four runners there were whoops of joy from the Africans in the stand. Over the final water jump Kip launched himself into the air and left Jipcho to fight, successfully, for the silver medal with Kantanen of Finland.

Today was also the final of the 200 metres sprint and this time all three Americans—Black, Smith and Burton—arrived at the starting line on time! Once again the smooth Valeri Borzov, the Russian scientist, proved his superiority and ran a beautiful race to record the exceptionally good time of 20·0 seconds. Afterwards Borzov refused to come to the Press conference and instead sent a message to the American journalists saying that he did not feel like turning up as they had been so insulting to him after the 100 metres. That is the sort of snub that I rather enjoy!

The German crowd had a marvellous time cheering a new 16-year-old heroine to a gold medal in the women's high jump. Ulrike Meyfarth is a schoolgirl from a town near Cologne. The German selectors did not really think that she was good enough for the Olympic Games but they put her into the team to gain experience. She did not need experience because throughout the long afternoon and evening she appeared quite unaffected by all the pressures. She jumped 4½ inches higher than she was jumping at the beginning of the season and eventually won the gold medal with a leap of 6 feet 3½ inches—equalling the world record.

At about the same time that young Miss Meyfarth was spinning her fairy-tale in the main stadium, Mark Spitz was putting the finishing touches to his fairy-tale story over in the swimming pool. Spitz swam the butterfly stage in the United States squad for the 4×100 metres medley relay—the event which brought the swimming events to a close at these Games. The American team's time of 3 min 48·2 sec was, of course, a new world record—the 30th world record to be set in this pool during the past eight days. And it brought the United States total of swimming gold medals to 18, of which Spitz himself has won seven. He said afterwards that he has now wiped out the memory of his defeats in Mexico four years ago. Before the Mexico Games he and his father promised that he would be first in five events. Today Spitz said: 'There were people ready to write me off as an arrogant brat who could not do the business when it came to the big ones. They were right in saying that I was a bit of a brat when I was younger but they were wrong about the other things. Maybe they will agree now. At the moment though I am in a bit of a trance.'

There is nothing like the memory of a traumatic defeat to stir an athlete to great things. Spitz has proved that victory can come out of defeat and that is something that both David Jenkins and David Bedford should remember.

While Spitz was celebrating the greatest haul of gold medals ever won by an athlete at a single Games another American swimmer, 16-year-old Rick Demont, was mourning the loss of the gold medal which he won yesterday in the 1500 metres free-style. Rick has suffered from asthma throughout his life and his doctor has prescribed a medicine to ward it off. Unfortunately, this medicine contains ephedrine which is one of the drugs banned by the Olympic Committee. Today it was announced that the medical commission of the I.O.C. had found traces of ephedrine in Rick Demont and he was therefore disqualified. Surely it should be possible for people who have to take certain drugs for their normal health to register the fact with the medical commission and get advice before their event?

11
'THEY'RE ALL PART OF OUR FAMILY—THE FAMILY OF MAN'

Tuesday/Wednesday, September 5th/6th

It was five o'clock on Tuesday morning in Munich, midnight on Monday evening in Toronto. For the past three hours the two cities had been connected by satellite relaying 'live' an Olympic side-show —the ice hockey match between Russia, the Olympic champions, and a Canadian team who, because they were professionals, had not been allowed to compete in the Winter Games. Now the second match of a needle series was being played in Toronto and transmitted 'live' to Europe. At the end of the transmission, Dagobert Lindlau, chief reporter of A.R.D., the first German television network, whose hobby is clay pigeon shooting, walked out of the Olympic Television Centre and turned right, passing the pedestrian gate at the end of Connolly Strasse, one of the streets of the Olympic Village. He heard a shot.

He looked at the guards and there was no reaction. He walked on thinking that one of the competitors in the shooting event had been lazy and had fired a 'cleaning' round. He went home to bed and slept for an hour before he was woken by a telephone call giving the news that Arab terrorists were in the Village, one Israeli was dead and a number were hostages. He did not sleep again for 44 hours.

In the Press Centre, the huge concrete housing estate half a mile from the Village, the news circulated slowly. All nights are late at the Olympic Games and Monday night was particularly late for most of the British Press. The Bedford story was over, Jenkins was out of the

400 metres, and on Tuesday nothing was scheduled to take place in the stadium. The Games were more than half over and at last there was an opportunity to relax. But some people were up early to attend the Mark Spitz Press conference scheduled for 9 a.m. They heard the news and came hammering on their colleagues' doors.

The Olympic Village, so we were told, was sealed off, all journalists banned. I put on a track suit and trotted across the bridge, past the hockey field, and up to the pedestrian gate at the north-west corner of the Village. It was locked but the guard invited me to climb over. No pass was asked for or shown.

Inside life was normal. Most athletes were unaware that war had come to the Village. There was the usual polyglot collection of people lounging around the plaza where the artificial stream rises in a marble slab. I headed south between the restaurant and the Rumanian quarters and then west along Connolly Strasse, past the Saudi Arabians and the Italians. Everything still seemed normal. Then, as the street turned, there was a barrier and a small crowd: New Zealanders (who lived just beyond the barrier), journalists, photographers and a film crew who said that they had climbed in over the fence at 7.00 a.m. Security men, unarmed, in blue trousers, white shirts and white holiday caps, guarded the barrier. A breathless New Zealand weight-lifter said that he had got to within thirty feet of the window of one of the flats in the Israeli building and had seen one of the Arab guerillas guarding the hostages and he had taken a photograph: 'did anyone want to buy it?'

High above, the balcony of the eleventh story of the Puerto Rican building was crowded with professional photographers with long bazooka-like lenses. A small walkie-talkie crackled with a report from a film crew man at the back of the Israeli building. A gunman, said the voice, could be seen at another window. It was not exclusive, nothing would be on this day.

A cameraman contrasted it with the day exactly two years before when he drove across the desert to Dawson's Field in Jordan to see the high-jacked airliners—the first media man on that scene. This scene in Munich was now being covered by 4000 journalists, 2000 television men and the most sophisticated electronic set-up in the world. The big 'live' camera on the high television tower overlooking the Olympic Stadium half a mile away had been turned round and was zoomed in on that one window in the Olympic

Village. It stayed on that one 'shot' throughout the day and the evening, sometimes close in on the window, sometimes a little wider looking at the whole Israeli building. It was a picture beamed, by line and satellite, all over the world.

All through that day and evening the people of the world stared at that window imagining what was going on inside in the minds of those Israeli sportsmen staring down the barrels of the guerillas' guns. This was the Olympic village in Munich on September 5th, 1972.

But officially, nothing has yet happened. At 10.45 a.m., five hours after the event, Dr. Manfred Schreiber, the police chief, addresses the first Press conference in the Olympic Press Centre. He reads his statement: one Israeli is dead, between nine and 26 are held as hostages, one of whom is known to be wounded. The *Egyptian* terrorists number perhaps six, perhaps 21. Before the translation into English and French is complete, Schreiber has left. No questions. The pattern has been set for the day.

In the Village the police have established a radio control van in the car park under the East German building and have roped off an area for a helicopter to land. Fifty yards away a man dives into the outdoor pool and a girl, with the figure of an athlete, sunbathes in a bikini.

Information was now passing instantaneously around the circle of people who ringed building 31, the Israeli Headquarters. It was a tight circle, no more than 70 yards in radius, and three dimensional because it had height—the top balconies of the East German and Puerto Rican buildings from which you could look down at an angle of 45° on building 31. That is why so many of the pictures that appeared next day showed the top of the negotiators heads and that strange light hat worn by the leader of the guerillas. You could stand at any point in the circle and receive information by word of mouth, by walkie talkie, from transistors tuned to the American Forces Network or to German stations, and from television sets in every flat. None of it was official and yet there was now a consensus of opinion about what had happened earlier in the day.

Just before dawn the guerillas had climbed the eight-foot wire mesh fence around the Village. They were dressed in track suits and carried sports bags inside which were their guns and grenades. They had been seen by some Post Office employees who took them for athletes returning from a party. I do not believe we shall ever learn the true story of what went on in those few chaotic minutes, at around 5.00 a.m., because most of those involved are now dead. But we do know that the Israeli weight-lifting coach, Tuvia Sokolovsky, was woken by shouting and banging in the corridor outside his rooms. He heard someone yelling: 'Boys, get out! Get out!' The terrorists were forcing their way into a room occupied by one of Sokolovsky's athletes, the weight-lifter, Yosef Romano. Romano was trying to hold the door shut whilst screaming warnings to his team mates. In the chaos two Israelis escaped and two were shot—Moshe Weinberg and Yosef Romano.

Half an hour later, the terrorists threw a statement of their demands, written on a sheet of paper, out of a first floor window. They asked for nothing less than the release of 200 Arab political prisoners held in Israel by 9.00 a.m.—only four hours ahead—at which time, they said, their Israeli hostages would be shot if their demands were not met. They also wanted a safe passage out of Germany for themselves.

During the next few hours, the German authorities set up operational headquarters in the administrative building of the Village. Those principally involved were the chief of police in Munich, Dr. Manfred Schreiber; the Federal Minister of the Interior, Hans-Dietrich Genscher; the Bavarian Minister of the Interior, Bruno Merk; the President of the West German Olympic Organising Committee, Herr Willi Daume; and the President of the International Olympic Committee, Mr. Avery Brundage. Later in the day the German Chancellor, Herr Willy Brandt, was also involved.

There are many unsolved problems in this affair and one of them is just how much influence Mr. Brundage had in the decisions taken that day. We certainly know that he had been informed of the guerilla attack at 6.00 a.m. and was in the village by half-past six. We certainly know that he did not pass the news on to his colleagues on the International Olympic Committee. Indeed, three crucial members of the Executive Board of the I.O.C. were on their way by plane to the yachting events at Kiel, before they heard about the attack. Mr. Brundage had done nothing to stop them catching that plane. Now, in conference with the German authorities, Brundage said that the whole I.O.C.—whom he had not consulted—would disapprove strongly if the Olympic hostages were allowed to be taken out of the Federal Republic of Germany. There must be, he asserted, no surrender to political blackmail. His determination, surprisingly, seems to have had an important effect on the German authorities. Dr. Schrieber, the Munich police chief, left one of the meetings in the administrative centre convinced that he would have the backing of both the Olympic and the Federal authorities if the situation came to a display of force. He at once sent out a call for sharpshooters.

Between 1.00 p.m. and 2.00 p.m., those watching the police activity at the back of the East German building reported that the police were arming themselves and then putting on new track suits. And the staff of the mobile operating room which was parked in the car park were putting on their white surgical smocks. So an attack was going to take place—it was going to happen here in the Olympic Village, in this idealistic meeting place for the youth of the world.

A sick joke circulated. Puma and Adidas are two German firms, sports goods manufacturers run by two warring brothers who fight for the privilege of clothing top athletes. The police were putting on new Puma tracksuits so, went the joke, Puma had won the contract for this event.

The second official Press conference at the Olympic Press Centre was held at 12.30 when Hans Klein, the bearded, charming Olympic Press chief, said that the guerillas' deadline, which had already been extended from 9.00 a.m. to 11.00 a.m. and then to mid-day, had been extended once again until 2.00 p.m. And he corrected that reference to *Egyptian* terrorists. It should have been Arab.

The high earth dyke between the Village and the television centre had now been cleared of spectators by the police. But the photographers were allowed to stay and they are now really organised with huge telescopic lenses mounted on tripods, chairs and step-ladders. Building 31 is less than 100 metres away and the photographers are skilled in focusing on a sprinter's face as he gets down in his blocks when they, the photographers, are beyond the finishing line. Nothing is likely to escape them. But one thing did. When they photographed the confrontation, outside the Israeli building, between the guerilla leader and German officials they did not see the grenade which the guerilla leader held in his hand, pin already drawn, just to emphasise that it was no good trying to pick him off.

Will Grimsley of Associated Press, the man who obtained that interview with Karl Schranz in Sapporo, spoke to a police lieutenant who said that thirty-eight German police volunteers were armed and ready to go in if there was no solution to the crisis by 5.00 p.m. Did this mean, we wondered, that they will go in *at* 5.00 p.m. Surely the police would wait for the cover of the darkness?

Inside the village there was now a large crowd of journalists. A Scottish press man had entered sandwiched between two Russian weight-lifters saying "niet" in broad Scots when asked for a pass. Kenny Moore, the American marathon runner, writing in the American magazine *Sports Illustrated*, tells far better than I can what it was like to be an ordinary competitor inside the village that day. In a superb article he wrote:

> At 3.30 p.m., I phoned a friend in the Press village 'Have you heard?' he asked. 'The Games are stopped.'
>
> 'Stopped? You mean postponed or cancelled?'
>
> 'Postponed for now. But they say it may be impossible to start them again.'
>
> I went back to my room, where my wife Bobbie was waiting, and I wept. I experienced level after level of grief; for my own event, the marathon, those years of preparation now useless; for the dead and doomed Israelis; and for the violated sanctuary of the Games. In Mexico and here the Village had been a refuge, admittedly imperfect, from a larger, seedier world in which individuals and governments refused to adhere to any humane code. For two weeks every four years we direct our kind of fanaticism into the essentially absurd activities of running, swimming and being beautiful on the balance beam. Yet even in the rage of competition we keep from hurting each other, and thereby demonstrate the meaning of civilisation. I shook and cried as that illusion, the strongest of my life, was shattered.

7.20 p.m. and it is getting dark. Klein goes to the microphone at the Olympic Press Centre and confirms that the 'wounded' hostage is dead and that his name is Yosef Romano. Just before 8.00 p.m. the drivers who wait for the world television network executives in the Lufthansa lounge of the Olympic television centre, rush up to the various network offices to report that Willy Brandt, the Federal Chancellor, has just walked through the lounge. At 8.00 p.m. Brandt makes a ministerial television statement to the German people. He says little except that there will be an enquiry into the security aspects of the whole affair. He says it sincerely, with pain.

All the networks want an interview with him. He says he will give one interview only—to the Israeli Television Service. They videotape the interview, Brandt speaking in English, and the Israelis make it available to all the other networks. Brandt then goes to the office of Robert Lembke, Head of the Olympic Television Consortium. Later a foreign network executive walks into Lembke's office to ask for details of the memorial service which has been announced for the next day and he discovers Brandt on the telephone to Egypt.

At 9.20 p.m. I am in the B.B.C.'s offices talking to an Irish radio reporter in Dublin when I hear helicopters fly over the television centre. It is nothing unusual: they have been doing that many times throughout the day. At 10.00 p.m. David Coleman is in the B.B.C. television studio which must be in line for the title of the smallest studio in the world. It is known as the 'Munchen Maus Haus'. He is rehearsing his opening lines and watching the monitor out of the corner of his eye—a monitor which is displaying the 'live' picture from the big camera on the television tower. It shows the outline of the Israeli buildings in the Olympic Village with a light or two burning. There are flashes. I am sitting next to David ready to speak about the atmosphere in the Village and I wonder whether the picture on our set is breaking up. Or could it be the flash bulbs of the photographers? They are always working, these photographers.

At 10.05 p.m. Coleman opens the programme by reporting that within the last hour there has been a complete security clamp down on the Village. He then introduces the Brandt video tape. I follow, reporting on the village atmosphere throughout the day and ending with a quote from Willie White, the Black American long jumper who was one of Mary Rand's rivals: 'They are part of us,' she had said, 'they're all part of our family—the family of man. It is horrible.'

Coleman takes over, speaking slowly because he is now being fed information through the earpiece in his right ear. Paul Fox, Controller of B.B.C. 1, is feeding the information cautiously from the next door control room. There has been enough rumour today and Fox sifts the information with care and Coleman chooses his words with care. The television monitor screen shows three helicopters, red belly lights flashing in the dark. The hostages and the Arab guerillas are aboard two of the helicopters. The two Ministers of the Interior, Hans-Dietrich Genscher (the Federal Minister) and

Dr. Bruno Merk (the State Minister) were in the third. The time was between 10.17 and 10.20 p.m.

Just before the programme ended at 11.00 p.m., David Coleman spoke of reports of shooting at Fuerstenfeldbruck air base.

At 11.30 p.m., the Reuter telex machine in the television centre spelled out confirmation from the official government spokesman in Bonn. The action at the air base had been successful; the hostages were safe and free; three guerillas were dead and the others were being pursued. In fact, this news had come from the police at the air base to Willy Brandt who was still in the television centre; and the Federal Chancellor had passed it on to his spokesman in Bonn who had, in his turn, relayed it back to Munich via the agencies. And from Munich it went out to the world.

All over Europe people who had watched throughout the day went to their beds thankful that the hostages were free. In Israel itself the Prime Minister, Mrs. Golda Meir, called for champagne and then she too went to her bed. Not until four hours later did the rejoicing stop.

It was just before 3 o'clock in the morning—Wednesday morning by now—when Hans Klein came to the microphone in the Olympic Press Centre and introduced the two Ministers of the Interior, Dr. Merk of Bavaria and Hans-Dietrich Genscher from Bonn. There was hardly room to move in the huge room, packed with more than 1000 journalists. Slowly, stage by stage, Dr. Merk went through the events of the day, repeating what we already knew, adding little that was fresh. Time after time he broke off for his story to be translated into English and then into French. One would think that at least the Germans would have ensured a high stanard of translation but anybody with a smattering of German or of French could tell that the interpretation into English was only telling half the story and even then was sometimes getting it wrong.

Eventually, after nearly an hour, Dr. Merk came to the events at Fuerstenfeldbruck and the horror was revealed. The helicopter carrying the two Ministers and the Chief of Police had landed first and the German officials hurried to the control tower. Less than ten minutes later the two helicopters carrying the Arab guerillas and their Israeli hostages had touched down about 40 yards from the main building. Some 150 yards away a Lufthansa Boeing was standing on the tarmac. Ostensibly the plane would then fly the terrorists and their hostages to their destination which the Arabs themselves had now said would be Cairo.

Two guerillas got out of each helicopter and forced the pilots and their co-pilots to climb down and stand with their hands behind their heads. Two terrorists stayed guarding the crews while the two others walked across the tarmac to inspect the Boeing. On their return, when they were halfway between the Boeing and the helicopter—when there were four terrorists in all on the tarmac—the police opened fire. The two terrorists guarding the helicopter crews were killed instantly and one of those crossing the tarmac was severely wounded. The fourth ran for the shelter of the helicopters and threw himself under one of them.

And then there was silence, silence which lasted for more than an hour. The hostages were still alive, bound together, waiting in those helicopters.

The police began to prepare a massive assault with armoured cars and automatic weapons. Perhaps one of the guerillas saw these preparations—who knows? What we do know is that shortly after midnight one of the guerillas leapt from one of the helicopters and threw a hand grenade back into it as he ran. There was a mighty explosion and the helicopter caught fire.

Dr. Merk told us that he believed the terrorists in the other helicopter then opened fire on their hostages and that we must assume that all the hostages had been killed—although it was just possible that one or two may have escaped from the flaming wreckage: 'and we shall not know until we have examined the wreckage of the burnt out helicopter.'

But there were no survivors amongst the hostages. The toll in Munich during the past twenty-four hours has been: two Israelis killed in the Olympic Village; nine Israeli hostages killed at the airfield; five terrorists killed at the airfield and three in custody. And one policeman, killed by terrorists bullets which struck the control tower. A total of seventeen men.

The carnage of Fuerstenfeldbruck leaves many unanswered questions.

Why was the security in the Olympic Village so slack? Israeli intelligence and the German authorities knew of the possibility of Arab terrorist action during the period of the Olympics. Yet security in the Olympic Village was slacker than in any other Olympic Village

I have ever known. It has been suggested that this was because of the protests of the world's Press who alleged that they could not get into the Village to do their job properly. But before this protest it was easy for anyone to get into the Village through the underground car park and certainly if you were wearing a track suit—as the Arab guerillas were—you were never questioned. Not once during the whole Games did I have to show my Village card. I have considerable sympathy with the German authorities who were trying to make these the friendly, smiling Games; to rid the world of its image of goose-stepping, disciplined, Germans. But why house the Israelis in a small building close to the perimeter fence? Why not house them on the top storeys of one of the skyscraper blocks in which it would have been easy to install guards on all lifts and stairs.

Why did the Germans decide to shoot it out?

Why did the Ministers of the Interior constantly reiterate the statement that if they had allowed the hostages to be taken out of Germany it would have been the equivalent of a death sentence?

Why were only five police marksmen used at the airport?

Why did the hostages suddenly demand to be taken to Cairo?

Why did they leave their citadel in the Olympic Village during the hours of darkness?

Why did the surviving terrorists, after two of their number had been killed and one wounded, suddenly decide, after more than an hour with their hostages in the helicopters, to end it all?

Why and how did the German police tell the political head of West Germany, Herr Willy Brandt, that all the hostages were safe and free?

I doubt if we shall ever know the answers to many of these questions: there is too much politics involved, too many people's reputations at stake. But there are some points which should be made.

It is impossible to lead a normal life and at the same time guard against acts of terrorism by men and women who have regard neither for their own lives nor for other people's lives.

It is not possible for sane and rational people who believe that life is precious to withstand the onslaught of fanatics unless they themselves become fanatics as the Israelis themselves have become on a number of occasions. Brute force, uncaring of life, can only be countered by brute force which is itself uncaring of life.

The Olympic Games have become the most publicised event in the world, watched by more people around the world than any other event with, perhaps, the sole exception of a moon walk. The Games stand as a symbol of peace and friendship between nations and are therefore wide open and will remain wide open to attack by fanatical groups.

The world is an increasingly violent place. There are now, surely, more people in the world prepared to sacrifice their lives in pursuit of the ideals they believe in than ever before in the history of the world.

The pattern has been set for future Games—indeed the pattern of Munich was surely set in Mexico where the students, knowing that the eyes of the world were focused on Mexico, took the opportunity of revolting against a dictatorial regime.

The next Olympic Games will be held in Montreal, a city which already has a history of the taking of hostages and of violence—both political and non-political.

Bullets and bombs have never provided a permanent solution.

* * *

On Wednesday morning, September 6th, we gathered in the stadium to remember the dead. The stands were packed and in the middle of the field, competitors and officials sat and stood. In the centre were the remaining members of the Israeli team, their grief in their faces and in their tears. Security men and women, armed, stood amongst them. The President of the Federal German Republic spoke. He said: 'In the last few hours it has become wholly evident to people in all parts of the world that hatred can only destroy. The victims of this new assault remind us that we must concentrate all our efforts on overcoming hatred and make it imperative to counter the fanaticism, which has horrified the world, with the desire for mutual understanding. The Olympic ideal has not been destroyed. We owe it more now than ever before. In the incident we have just experienced, no line divides North and South, East and West. Here the division is between the brotherhood of all men who desire peace and those who place in jeopardy the things which make life worth living. Life needs reconciliation and reconciliation must not fall victim to terror.'

And then spoke Avery Brundage, 84-year-old, tired and angry. He said: '. . . sadly in this imperfect world, the greater and the more important the Olympic Games become the more they are open to commercial, political and now criminal pressure. The Games of the XXth Olympiad have been subjected to two savage attacks. We lost the Rhodesian battle against naked political blackmail. We have only the strength of a great ideal. . . . The Games must go on and we must continue our efforts to keep them clean, pure and honest, and try to extend the sportsmanship of the athletic field into other areas.'

The President of the Federal German Republic had struck a chord in our hearts, had made us feel that indeed 'the brotherhood of all men who desire peace' must continue and be reaffirmed. And then Avery Brundage equated the death of those hostages with his Committee room battle over Rhodesia. Seldom has a man so misjudged the feelings of the world.

12
'BUT WHO GETS ALL THE PUBLICITY?'

Thursday, September 7th

After the events of the past two days, 80,000 people in the Olympic stadium are determined that nobody else is going to sully the Olympic spirit. So when Vince Matthews and Wayne Collett, the gold and silver medallists in the 400 metres final today, stood on the victory rostrum while their anthem was being played with their hands on their hips and gently chatting, the crowd gave them the 'bird'.

Poor Vince Matthews, who is as thick as a pair of gumboots, did not really know what he was doing. Neither of them would come to the traditional Press conference for medallists, but then Matthews was cornered down in the bowels of this immense stadium by a bunch of journalists who remembered that incident in Mexico four years ago after Tommie Smith and John Carlos, both black American athletes, had won medals in the 200 metres. They greeted the American flag with the Black Power salute—the raised clenched fist. And the International Olympic Committee were so annoyed that these two athletes had introduced politics into the Games again that they insisted that the American team management take disciplinary action. They did. Smith and Carlos were sent home in disgrace and became martyrs—hailed by one part of American society as men who had the courage to proclaim their beliefs.

But today Vince Matthews was a very confused person: 'If we had wanted to make a Black Power demonstration we could have done a much better job.' He denied that he meant to be disrespectful, saying merely that he can never keep still—especially after he has run a race. But of course Wayne Collett, a very intelligent man, was fully aware of what was going on. Some minutes after the ceremony he walked from the presentation area towards the athletes' tunnel and this huge crowd, always quick to spot anything that goes on in the stadium, saw him and howled. He replied—with the Black Power salute. These two utterly misjudged the mood here in the stadium as—to be truthful—Avery Brundage did yesterday. Nobody wants any more intrusion—everybody yearns for tolerance and peace—and woe betide anybody who brings any divisive element into the Olympic arena.

Let us turn to a happier subject—Sheila Carey. Four years ago as Sheila Taylor, a complete unknown, she came fourth in the 800 metres final in Mexico, beating the more fancied British girls. This year she was out of the Olympic team, having come last in the final trials of the 1500 metres. As her coach, John Anderson, says—he coaches David Jenkins as well—'when Sheila is bad she is paralytically bad'.

But the selectors gave her another opportunity and she had to run for the last place in the Olympic team against Rita Ridley, the British record holder over 1500 metres, and Norine Braithwaite, daughter of Bob—the clay pigeon gold medallist in Mexico. She won that trial, came to Munich, and today ran brilliantly in the semi-finals of the 1500 metres to qualify for a place in the final with a new British record of 4 min 7·4 sec, which is more than five seconds faster, say about 30 yards faster, than the record stood last week. She has a chance of a medal in the final because she is a very tough girl, but it is impossible to think that it will be the gold medal because Ludmilla Bragina, a slight, 29-year-old Russian woman, the world record holder before the Games, has beaten her own world record in both the heats and semi-finals and now holds it at 4 min 5·1 sec.

After today's heats of the 5000 metres, Britain are the only country with three runners in the final and all of them must have a chance of getting amongst the medals. Dave Bedford, running in the first heat, had us all worried for the first eight laps. The pace was not fast and he was doing absolutely nothing about speeding it up—a very dangerous situation for a man who has no finish. But then with just under 3000 metres to go he suddenly took off and ran the next lap in a cool 60 seconds and followed it with two more laps in 61 seconds.

That really split the field. This is the way that many people wanted him to run the 10,000 metres last Sunday. Let others do the work for the first half of the race—and plenty of them would have done so in a final—and then from about halfway explode with three or four laps that would crucify the opposition. Today the only man that could equal Dave was Mohamed Gammoudi, the reigning Olympic champion at this distance. Dave and Gammoudi finished together, comfortably ahead of the rest of the field, in a time of 13 min 49·8 sec.

It was a comfortable and sensible way of qualifying for the final on Sunday. Much more sensible than the way Ian McCafferty qualified in his heat. There are five heats and only the first two in each heat are certain to qualify—with another four, those with the fastest times, also getting to the final. With 500 metres still to run there was a big bunch of runners still in contention in McCafferty's heat and he was lying a comfortable third. But then at the bell, everybody swept past him and he was thoroughly boxed in, all chance apparently gone. But as they hit the back straight, Ian accelerated to pass the whole field and from that moment on there was never any doubt. His winning time was 13 min 38·2 sec. Ian Stewart qualified comfortably in heat four together with Juha Vaatainen of Finland, the European champion at this distance.

This was only Vaatainen's second race this year because he has been troubled with a knee injury. Vaatainen, an upright Edwardian looking figure, is really the man who started the Finnish revival in the middle and long distance events. He is a man who does not fit into any system yet a wise system, as run by the Finns, takes care of him too. I find his politics rather odd: he is on the extreme right, but then I suppose that makes him his own man, like Enoch Powell. Certainly you could not find any athlete in Munich who is more his own man. He knew that after winning both the 5000 and 10,000 metres at the European championships in Helsinki last year, he would be the ante-post favourite for both these events at these Games. He knew the pressures—that the world's Press would want to talk to him and all Finland to shake him by the hand.

But he was going to go about his preparation in his own way and his way was to accept graciously the prize given by a leading Finnish newspaper for the outstanding Finnish athlete in the European championships—a month in Kenya, which Juha extended to two months. In December he came home to Oalu, a town on the edge of Lapland, and campaigned for two weeks as a candidate in the general election. He ran from speech to speech and then, a week before polling day, flew off to Brazil to run in the New Year's Eve Round-the-Houses Race in Sao Paulo. He did not run well and he lost the election!

Then he went to Portugal to live simply in a remote primitive community. 'I am a school teacher,' he said, 'without a job. I am a free man. Avery Brundage would never believe how little money I need for my daily sleeping and eating.'

And then in the spring he went back to Finland, to the freedom of the forests. But still he did not compete. In fact the only race he has run this year, a 5000 metres in the slow time of 14 min 3 sec, was in the Finnish championships in August—championships which took place in the town of Joensu. Thirty-seven thousand people live there and on the three days of the championships 33,000 paid to get in to the stadium! That is a measure of the popularity of athletics in Finland.

So we have a spectacular line-up for the 5000 metres final on Sunday: Gammoudi of Tunisia, the reigning champion; Puttemans of Belgium, the silver medallist in the 10,000 metres; Steve Prefontaine of the United States whom Ron Clarke has named as the likely winner; Vaatainen and Viren of Finland; Sviridov of Russia; Alvarez and Haro of Spain; and three British runners. I hope that Dave will run the final in the same fashion as he ran the heat today —let somebody else make the early pace and then try to destroy the field with some fast laps in the middle.

There is some talk of the three British runners helping each other tactically in the final on Sunday but the people who say this are utterly unaware of an athlete's real feelings—he is running for himself and not as a member of a team for his country. Besides, there is no love lost between the two Scots, McCafferty and Stewart, and Dave the Englishman. And it has not anything to do with Scotland versus England. Ian Stewart, after all, is a European champion both indoors and out, and also the Commonwealth Games gold medallist. He, as he points out, has proved himself in big competition while Dave Bedford has never won a major international title on the track. But who, asks Ian, gets all the publicity? Athletes do like to be recognised, you know.

The Irish also brought their troubles to the Olympic arena today, but they did it in such a delightful fashion that not many people can take offence. Four cyclists from the Republic of Ireland and members of the National Cycling Federation of Ireland, which is not recognised by the international governing body, hid themselves in a ditch yesterday morning intent on joining in the 125 mile road race. They stayed there for hour after hour, unaware that the race had been postponed for 24 hours because of the memorial service in the stadium. But they were back at their posts early this morning and, when the race came past them, they joined in. Wearing green, orange, and white striped jerseys and riding new bikes they managed to baffle the police and the television commentators. Indeed after ten miles, one of them, with the magnificent name of Batty Flynn, was leading the race and the bemused TV commentators were referring to him as 'an unknown Dutchman'. The official Irish team is made up of three Dubliners and one Ulsterman, Noel Taggart. The renegade Irish singled out Taggart and rode him into a ditch and then started distributing pamphlets about the political situation in Northern Ireland! All four 'unofficial' Irishmen were arrested—and so were their bikes—but despite the protests of the official Irish team manager the German police let them go.

13
WHAT HAPPENED?–'YOU TELL ME!'

Friday/Saturday, September 8th/9th

I wish for three things: that committees would not be so pompous; that the organisers would banish the computer from all future Games; and that whoever plans the track and field programme would redistribute the goods. On Sunday we shall have nine finals in the stadium and that is just too many—rather like a feast at which you are forced to eat too much. It means that these two days have too many preliminary heats and not enough finals.

But first the pompous committee: naturally enough it is the International Olympic Committee to whom I refer. On Friday they issued the following Press release: 'After the insulting display of the two American athletes given in the stadium on September 7th, when they were awarded their gold and silver medals for the 400 metre event, the Executive Board decided that, being the second time that the United States Olympic Committee had permitted such occurrences on the Olympic athletic field, these two athletes had broken Rule 26, Paragraph 1, in respect of the traditional Olympic spirit and ethic and would, therefore, be eliminated from taking part in any future Olympic competition. If such a performance should happen in the future the medals would be withheld from the athletes in question. The United States National Olympic Committee has apologised and has been cautioned about future competitors.'

If ever I saw a statement that is not in keeping with the Olympic spirit that is it. The Olympic Games is supposed to be about *athletes* taking part not about pompous nationalistic victory ceremonies with their flag waving and national anthems. Pray, how is it possible for the United States Olympic Committee, a bunch of rather old, right-wing white men to have any control whatsoever over some of the black athletes?

What really irks me is that in 1968 the International Olympic Committee made a rule that no athlete who lives at normal altitudes should be allowed to spend more than four weeks in a high altitude training camp in the period before the Games. On my way to Mexico City I called at the American team's high altitude training camp at Lake Tahoe and there I discovered that some of their athletes had been training at altitude for three months. When I rang up the Chairman of the U.S. Olympic Committee and asked him why they were purposely breaking the rule, all he could say was: 'What are you, a detective?'

So they are quite prepared to break rules that really matter and the International Olympic Committee take no action whatsoever. But when it comes to the case of a victory ceremony—which many people believe should be abolished—then the International Olympic Committee take punitive action

But let us turn to that computer. The heats of all the events are supposed to be seeded and the seeding is based on the athletes' fastest time in the event before the Games. Well, Jim Ryun is the world record holder for the 1500 metres and for the mile and this year he has run a mile in 3 min 52·8 sec, faster than anyone else in the world. But the wretched computer cannot tell the difference between a mile time and a 1500 metres time and it assumed that this was a very slow time for 1500 metres (in fact it's the equivalent of approximately 3 min 36 sec for the 1500 metres, faster than anyone has run this year.) So, as far as the computer was concerned, Ryun was no more than cannon fodder to be placed in one of the heats that the computer imagined would be won by one of the stars like Kip Keino. And that is what the computer did—put Keino and Ryun in the same heat!

What a tragedy it was for Ryun. He was taking it fairly easily at the back of the field until he came into the finishing straight with 500 metres still to run. He came out to clear the bunched field and as he did so Billy Fordjour, of Ghana, caught him with a foot and both of them crashed to the ground. For a couple of seconds I thought that Ryun had knocked himself out on the kerb but then he was up and chasing the field. But it was an impossible task and poor Jim, the silver medallist in Mexico, is not even through to the semi-finals.

Disaster after disaster seems to follow this American team. They cannot get their sprinters to the starting line in time; they lose the pole vault because the International Amateur Athletic Federation take away their advanced technology poles; the heart of their 400 metres relay team, Vince Matthews and Wayne Collett, have been barred from any further competition; and now Jim Ryun, the fastest man in the world over 1500 metres, has crashed out of the Olympics. Is it just a run of bad luck? Is it bad team management? Or is it, as I believe, that the team is divided amongst itself just as American society is divided, waging an internal war. I do not think there is any doubt that an unhappy society produces an unhappy team.

Jim Ryun did not know what happened to him. 'You tell me,' he said when I saw him afterwards. 'Everything was going well and the next thing I was on the ground.' It is amazing that he ever got up and started to run again but then he is a man who is constantly fighting battles.

If there had been an Olympic Games in 1966 or 1967 he would have been a certainty for a gold medal. In those years he brought the world mile record down to 3 min 51·1 sec and the 1500 metres world record down to 3 min 33·1 sec—and that is where they remain five years later. But then in Olympic year, 1968, he caught glandular fever, a really horrible, lowering, disease. Yet he went up to altitude in Mexico City and won a silver medal behind the man who was born at altitude, Kip Keino.

I think that might have satisfied him, but then early in 1969, he got married. His wife rather liked the idea of travelling the world and seeing glamorous places in the wake of her husband Jim. So Jim ran and he ran well. Until something snapped, something in his mind, and he dropped out of the American National championships after only two laps. He did not compete again for another eighteen months, but then that urge for travel gripped the Ryun family again and he was off on the indoor circuits. He came to Europe and finished last to Kip Keino in a mile in Stockholm, running the truly Victorian time of 4 min 18 sec. He had asthma and allergies and moved home from Oregon to California to try to avoid them, and slowly things improved and he made the American team for Munich. And then when he gets here the computer makes that ridiculous mistake and puts him in the same heat as Kip Keino—the gold and silver medallist of 1968 running together.

Let us move on to Saturday and that slip of a woman, the Russian, Ludmilla Bragina—only 7 stone 12 pounds and 5 feet 5 inches tall. She is the most phenomenal distance runner I have ever seen. At the beginning of the year the world record for the 1500 metres stood at 4 min 9·6 sec—say about 4 min 30 sec for the mile. But now this tiny 29-year-old Russian, who confesses to no job, no hobby, no home town, has won a gold medal and lowered the record to an incredible 4 min 1·4 sec, which Arnold Strode Jackson, an octogenarian, would have respected when he won his gold medal in Stockholm in 1912. Indeed, Miss Bragina would have beaten every one of the men in the decathlon 1500 metres and those decathletes call themselves the finest all-round athletes in the world. So, for that matter, would Sheila Carey, who came fifth in the 1500 metres final with yet another British record of 4 min 4·8 sec—almost eight seconds, say 50 yards, faster than Rita Ridley's record set up in the European championships last summer.

The two Dutch girls, Keizer and Boxen, set a fast early pace (62·5 sec and 67·5 sec) before Comrade Bragina took over and immediately opened an unassailable gap. Sheila Carey took up the chase but she could not hold her stride for a full two laps and was overtaken on the back straight of the last lap. But just to come fifth in such a time was a most courageous performance by this 26-year-old Coventry girl.

If Irish athletes will excuse me, there are not more than a dozen Irish men, excluding Ronnie Delany (the Olympic 1500 metre champion of 1956), who could run faster than either Miss Bragina or Mrs. Carey. And that information came to me from an Irish journalist who wishes to remain anonymous!

In the relays the British girls are through to the final, although they have no hope of a medal in either the 4 × 100 metres or the 4 × 400 metres. The sprinters came fourth in their heat with a time of 43·8 seconds, a second slower than the Cubans or the Russians. And the 400 metres girls were lucky to qualify for the final. They were lying a bad fifth when the Polish girls dropped the baton, picked it up again and ran off the track under the mistaken impression that they would be automatically disqualified.

Three years ago a British 400 metres quartet won a European

title, but that was when Lillian Board was alive. On a warm night in Athens in 1969 she ran the greatest race of her life, taking over just behind Colette Besson—the French girl who so unexpectedly beat her in the Mexico Games—and won by the thickness of a running vest.

The British men failed to qualify for the final in their sprint relay, coming sixth in 39·5 seconds. But the 4 × 400 metres men—Martin Reynolds, Alan Pascoe, David Hemery and David Jenkins—have an exceptionally good chance of a silver medal tomorrow thanks to the severity with which the International Olympic Committee have treated the American 400 metre runners.

I must confess to a prejudice against the heavy field events because, without exception, all the top men are taking anabolic steroids to increase their weight. There is nothing illegal about this, because the I.O.C. have not banned steroids for the simple reason that they know there is no adequate way of testing a person quickly and cheaply. The Marquess of Exeter, the President of the International Amateur Athletic Federation, told me that he reckons that the steroid problem will be beaten in six months. But until such a time and until all the heavy men have shed the weight they have been putting on with the aid of steroids, these events, traditional though they may be, should be left out of the athletics programme.

I seem to be in a thoroughly complaining mood today so let me just end with another complaint—about the marathon. I have run over the course (not all in one go—I took three days to do it!) and I would dearly like to see the race itself, but if I do follow it tomorrow that means that I miss all the other eight finals including the 5000 metres and the 1500 metres. Kip Keino complains about those two events clashing on the same day and I complain about them clashing with the marathon. Someone ought to organise a Games in which there is one centrepiece event every day. But who would choose which event should be the centrepiece!

14
'YOU CAN RUN A GREAT RACE WITH THAT MUSIC IN YOUR HEAD'

Sunday, September 10th

This was Finland's day. Lasse Viren, the 23-year-old policeman, won the 5000 metres, thus completing the first long distance Olympic track double since the great days of Vladimir Kuts in 1956. And then another Finn, the impeccable Pekka Vasala added to their triumph by taking the 1500 metres from Kip Keino. So now Finnish athletes have won gold medals in the 1500 metres, the 5000 metres, the 10,000 metres and a bronze medal in the 3000 metres steeplechase. It is just like the old days for them, the days between the wars when they won thirty out of the possible sixty medals in these four events.

What a nation of runners they are, headed by a President, Kekkonen, who was once a very good high jumper and who was commandant of the Finnish team in the 1936 Games. He is over 70 now and the only Head of State in the world who has been seen taking his early morning run in Central Park, New York—much to the consternation of the New York police who could not keep up with him. And when it gets too cold to run in the Finnish winter, he goes cross-country skiing, doing more than 400 miles on his skis every winter. When the Head of State sets such an example, is it surprising that they have such great runners?

There are only four and a half million of them living in a vast land, a land of lakes and forests, and I have always had a great affinity for the people that live in that land. It is my favourite country—after Britain. In my youth I read about those flying Finns like Paavo Nurmi and Willy Ritola—who looked like, and was known as, 'The Wolf'. And Iso-Hollo, the great steeplechaser, and Lauri Lehtinen, the 5000 metres man: how these names roll off the tongue and what great athletes they were. A runner needs to get into the right mood, to steel his will, to think of guts and glory, and I used the music of a Finnish composer, Sibelius, to get me in the right mood. The last movement of the Fifth Symphony—it is magnificent—you can run a great race with that music in your head.

But it has not been easy for them. After the last war—in which they suffered as much as any country—the rest of the world caught and passed them, and they did not win a single medal on the track until these Games here in Munich. They felt the famine and they did something about it—they made a five-year plan and imported Arthur Lydiard, the New Zealand coach of Peter Snell and Murray Halberg, and he noticed that they seemed to have lost their essential Finnish character. They were trying to copy the world and do all their training on the track: and there are plenty of those—at least ten in a Finnish town the size of Barnsley. He sent them out into the forests again, come snow or rain, and there they rediscovered their spirit.

Those people who have watched these races on television must have noticed how Vasala and Viren run—lightly, above the ground, as if gravity hardly exists. They are relaxed, floating down the track. And that is the quality that I believe all the great champions of Munich have: like Valeri Borzov, the smoothest and most balanced sprinter I have ever seen. And like John Akii-Bua who beat David Hemery. And like Kip Keino who won the silver in the 1500 metres today—Kip of the flowing stride, floating over the track, a smile on his face.

These are the great athletes—those who, amidst all the tension that we hear so much about, can still relax and enjoy themselves. It is a quality that we would do well to learn in Britain. It is the quality, the frame of mind, which treats sport as only a part of life—not the be-all and end-all of existence. That surely is the essence of sport and the Finns have it and live by it. No country is under more apparent pressure—they love the freedom of the West and yet they have a long border with Russia. If they took it all too seriously, their life would not be worth living. But they do not take it at all too seriously: they do not pursue material wealth; instead they take to the lakes and forests of their country where their athletes found the mental, spiritual and physical strength to win here in Munich.

Thirteen men lined up for the final of the 5000 metres and one of them was hardly recognisable. It was Dave Bedford, *sans* beard and moustache (he shaved them off in order to smuggle himself back into England) and *sans* his flowing locks. Maybe it was an attempt to give himself a new personality—certainly something of the old Dave was lacking. And there was something lacking in the race. As my colleague, John Rodda, put it so well in his article in *The Guardian*: 'The 5000 metres, billed as one of the richest races in the Games, had the ingredients: but something went wrong in the cooking.'

Maybe they were all waiting for Dave to make the pace and Dave was determined that he was not going to do so. They dawdled and dithered, first one taking the lead and then another while those behind bunched up and used their arms to give themselves space. Ron Clarke's world record was going to be safe today. Even when Dave did go to the front, looking like an 18-year-old, there was no resolve in his running. First it was Sviridov of Russia, then McCafferty, then Viren himself, then Alvarez of Spain—but still nobody had any sense of urgency.

At last, when there were only four laps still to go the stocky American, Steve Prefontaine, his long blond hair flowing out behind him, starts a long powerful stride for home. Ian Stewart, Dave Bedford and Lasse Viren are with him but Bedford is not there for long. On the back straight with two and a half laps to go the race was between Prefontaine, Viren, Puttemans of Belgium, Gammoudi of Tunisia and Ian Stewart of Britain. There was nothing sudden about the increase in the pace, but now they really were flying. One lap later and Stewart was dropped. At the bell the American was still in the lead, chunky and powerful, followed by the lean and smooth Viren and the dark, silky Gammoudi, defending the title which he won in Mexico. The Finn does not have a kick but he builds up a flowing pace that can destroy the greatest runners. And so he did, coming home to win by a good 6 yards from Gammoudi with Ian Stewart picking up pace in the finishing straight and overhauling the fast tiring Prefontaine to snatch the bronze medal. It was not the greatest 5000 metres that I have seen but what more can you ask of a man than that he should win two of the prime events in the Olympic Games. That is what Lasse Viren, the quiet policeman from Finland, has done and we shall see him many more times, and by the time that his athletic career has finished the record books will have been rewritten.

The 1500 metres did have a pacemaker and a British runner at that—Brendan Foster, who knows that he must make his strength tell. He went straight to the front but there was not the same power in his pace as there had been in the heats and the semi-finals. With two laps to go the defending champion, Kip Keino, slipped smoothly into the lead but he too seemed to have lost the reach of that silky stride. How I remember the way that he destroyed Jim Ryun at the same stage of the same race four years ago. Today he made his move at the same place but it was not positive enough and the distinguished, bearded Finn, Pekka Vasala, slipped in behind, slip-streaming the Kenyan for a lap and three-quarters until Vasala came off the last bend and surged into the lead. Vasala's time was 3 min. 36·3 sec—nearly 1½ seconds outside Keino's Olympic record set in 1968. Rod Dixon of New Zealand came through to take the bronze medal and I have never seen a man so delighted. Early in the week he had sprained his ankle when jumping over a fence and he thought he would never be able to compete. To get through a hard heat and semi-final and to come through this final and win a medal is really a great achievement for the young New Zealander who has no international experience at all.

One other tribute—to Brendan Foster. This 24-year-old school teacher from County Durham has certainly got guts. He won a bronze medal at the Commonwealth Games and at the European championships and now he has a fifth place in the Olympic 1500 metres. He is never afraid to make the pace and he never gives up. If only his guts and competitive spirit were aligned with Dave Bedford's natural ability then what an athlete we should see—a mile in under 3 minutes 50 seconds and a 5000 metres approaching 13 minutes.

While all this was going on in the stadium, the marathon runners were making their tortuous way through Munich and its suburbs. Ron Hill, clad in a silvered string vest, silver shorts and silver shoes (designed to reflect the heat), was in the leading bunch after 10 kilometres (just over six miles). But then, as the course wound through paths in the grounds of Nymphenburg Castle, he dropped steadily back, and the tall moustached American, Frank Shorter (who was born in Munich when his father, an army doctor, was stationed here twenty-four years ago), sweating profusely but moving easily, went to the front and started to build a long and commanding lead.

I had thought that with this class of field and on this flat and interesting course, this marathon was bound to produce a new world best time but today was too sultry and humid for distance running. How they must have suffered as they ran over the lonely paths of the Englischgarten, a linear park alongside the river. It is hard to imagine the thoughts of a man out in front in an Olympic marathon, wondering whether he can last the distance, wondering whether he has not misjudged his efforts like Dorando Pietri did in 1908 or Etienne Gailly in 1948. Both these men led into the stadium but Dorando was disqualified for receiving assistance when he collapsed just before the finishing line and Gailly was passed by two other competitors on the very last lap.

But the tall, thin American hung on and it was he whom we expected to see coming through the tunnel at the bottom of the finishing straight. Instead we saw a fresh looking runner in yellow shorts burst out of the tunnel and start the final lap looking as fresh as a man who has only run half a mile. And indeed that is all he had run, for this was a German student, Norbert Sudhaus, who did it for a joke and thus deprived Shorter of what must surely be a marathon runner's greatest moment—the moment when he comes into the stadium to receive the acclaim of the crowds, the acclaim due to a man who has triumphed in the cruellest event in the Olympic programme. Little Karel Lismont, the European champion from Belgium, a man who has never before been beaten in the marathon, came second and the reigning chamipion, Mamo Wolde of Ethopia, was third. Kenny Moore of America was fourth and another American, Jack Bacheler, ninth. The old jibe that the Americans have lost the use of their legs no longer holds true. So many new movements start in the States and I believe that they have gone through the full cycle of falling in and out of love with the motor car and that they are now, in droves, taking to the bicycles and to their feet. If there was a team gold medal in the marathon, as there is in the Three Day Event, then America would have won it.

Ron Hill was sixth, just in front of Don MacGregor, but what a disappointed man he was. He has trained every day of his life (twice on weekdays) since 1964, aiming for an Olympic gold medal and now it has eluded him. Perhaps it was the humidity, perhaps it was that unfamiliar and uncomfortable looking silver outfit. But in my opinion it was probably due to the fact that he spent three weeks training at altitude in St. Moritz. I do not believe it was the altitude which affected him as much as the unfamiliar training conditions. On some days he was running for nearly three hours and at least an hour of his training was over the mountains. I am sure that this is marvellous training, but only in the build-up period, not in those vital three weeks just before the Olympic Games. What one needs in those last weeks is a regime which you have tried and tested and which is utterly familiar to your mind and your body. Ron is a man who loves to run and maybe he will go on until Montreal. He will be 37 years old then but that is not too old for an event that requires such stamina.

The last event of the track and field programme brought a silver medal to the British 4 × 400 metres relay team—Martin Reynolds, Alan Pascoe, David Hemery and David Jenkins. Martin and Alan kept the team in contact with the leaders and then David Hemery took them into fourth place with a brilliant lap in 44·9 seconds. He handed over to Jenkins who did not seem to be making up much ground on the back straight but when they came to the finishing straight, Karl Honz of Germany tied up cruelly and the lithe Julius Sang of Kenya swept into the lead with Jenkins powering past both the German and the Frenchman to come second in a new British record of 3 min 0·5 sec. It was a great finale to David Hemery's Olympic career—the farewell of a perfect gentleman of the track. And it was some consolation to David Jenkins for his defeat in the 400 metres semi-final.

Strangely enough if both the Davids had adopted the same tactics in their individual races as they did today, then they might both have done better. They said afterwards that at a team meeting last night they discussed tactics for the final today and realised that all of them had noticed that the runners who 'floated' down the back straight were the ones who recorded the fastest times. So that was their tactic today. As Jenkins said: 'We all planned to cruise down the back straight and then hit the home straight as hard as we could. I felt strong today, much better than the semi-final. . . .'

So what is the final British score on the track? One gold medal from Mary Peters, one silver medal from the relay team and two bronze medals from David Hemery and Ian Stewart.

If you want to make a medal table, then that puts Britain in seventh place. But such tables are nonsense and certainly not in accord with Olympic tradition. They are entirely unofficial, compiled by the news agencies because they know that there is a world-wide demand for them. They mean absolutely nothing to the athletes in the Olympic Village. Not one single athlete who has ever won a medal, and to whom I have talked, feels that he is out there in the Olympic stadium running for his country. He is just trying to prove something to himself and this is that he—or she for that matter—is the best in the world at that event on one particular day in 1972.

I remember talking to Herb Elliott after he had won his gold medal in Rome in 1960 and asking him: 'When were you first aware that you were wearing an Australian vest and that many people thought you were running for your country?' And he replied: 'Not until they started to play the national anthem and I turned towards the flag. Only then did it affect me.'

I am afraid that I cannot remember what I felt like on the victory rostrum in 1956. Immediately after the race I was disqualified and it was not until all the events were over in the stadium that the jury were able to meet, hear the evidence and then reinstate me. So the medal ceremony was postponed until the next day at 2.45. That morning Desmond Hackett of the *Daily Express* telephoned me in the Olympic Village and invited me to lunch with the British Press. There were thirteen members of the British Press present and we started lunch by having a drink in the bar. Mine was a gin and tonic—a double as I discovered later. But of course every member of the Press had to buy a round so at 2.42 precisely, after 13 double gins and tonic and with no food someone realised I had to be on the rostrum in three minutes! How we made it I do not know but I do know that Desmond swears that the member of the International Olympic Committee who presented the medals had to lasso me because I was swaying around so much!

But to get back to my point: all this nationalism and flag waving and medal tables are utterly out of keeping with the true spirit of the Games. They must go, and at last there are many people admitting that fact. There is even a majority on the aristocratic International Olympic Committee who believe that all the marching of teams, raising of flags and national anthems, should be done away with. But a plain majority is not enough—there has to be a two-thirds majority to get the regulations changed.

Yet I must confess that since I moved off the track into the Press Box, I have found myself getting more nationalistic. The only time when I have found myself standing on my desk in the swimming stadium and yelling like a dervish was when Anita Lonsbrough won her gold medal in 1960. I did not do it here for Mark Spitz or Shane Gould. They are greater swimmers than Anita ever was, but they did not come from my country. So we are all in this—getting greater pleasure from the athletes from our own country than we do from those of other countries. I suppose it is only human nature but it is utterly false and contrary to the idealism behind this Olympic movement—which should be a meeting-place for the youth of the world regardless of race, creed or national origin. George Orwell, that prophet of so much that is wrong with the world, once wrote about 'the lunatic modern habit of identifying oneself with large power units and seeing everything in terms of competitive prestige'.

Indeed it is lunatic and it will ruin the Games.

* * *

So the track and field competition is over, and weary to my heart with so much excitement and emotion I went back to the Press Centre for a last late supper. Halfway through the meal a colleague came running into the restaurant saying: 'There is shooting in the Village.' We dashed out to the office of Hans Klein, the Olympic Press chief, and there the story began to unfold. Indeed, shots had been heard; indeed a policeman in the Village had seen a man with a revolver but had done nothing more than report the fact to his superiors; indeed there was one person dead. But then the story began to come together. The dead youth had fallen from a flag pole while trying to steal an Olympic flag and had broken his neck. And the noise of the shots? Nobody did discover whether this was the slamming of doors in the high wind that raked the Village that night or whether it was the popping of champagne corks in the French headquarters. What we do know, with certainty, is that all our nerves are on edge.

15
'HE WAS TWENTY-TWO YEARS OLD AND WHITE AND LOOKED THE PART'

by John Rafferty

The boxing in Munich inevitably centred round the winning of the heavyweight gold medal. Beforehand the medal had been freely valued at a million dollars and if the latest United States white hope Duane David Bobick were to win it then the value would be increased to pounds. It was reported that a consortium had already been formed to commercialise him.

Bobick, a Quartermaster third class in the United States Navy, was one of a family of twelve. He was reckoned after fifty-nine straight wins to be as near a certainty as one could be in the intense competition of the Olympic Games. He had boxed in two weight classes and his record read 91 fights, 82 wins, 58 knock outs. He was 22 years old and white and looked the part.

And then into the scene pushed the tall handsome Cuban, Teofilo Stevenson, who had taken Bobick to a close decision in the Pan-American championships. He came to the Games Village confident that he would beat Bobick and indeed that he would stop him. When the draw was made there was the exciting prospect of these two better-than-average heavyweights meeting in the second round.

Bobick was first to show and he fought the clever Russian, Yuri Nesterov, who had been switched into heavyweight when the original entrant had been badly beaten by Bobick. The United States sailor turned out to be a hard, tough fighter in the barging style of Bugner. He took the clever stuff that Nesterov threw at him and banged away, weakening him and by sheer persistence and strength took a comfortable verdict.

Teofilo Stevenson was more elegant in beating an unfortunate Pole, Denderys. With casual grace he hit him with as many good right hand punches as one could hope to see and had him so battered before the first round was half over that the referee stopped the fight. The way was clear for the big fight of the tournament: Bobick, the white hope, against Stevenson from Cuba, where professional boxing is banned.

The astonishing aspect of the Munich boxing was that every session was sold out—even the first one which is normally not well attended. There was a furious market for tickets for the big heavyweight night. Bobick went into the round still marked from his hard fight with the Russian, Nesterov. He had a puffiness under his left eye which was soon a target for the right hand of Stevenson. The Cuban stood upright and met Bobick as he bored in and hurt him with mighty punches.

The sailor stepped up the pace and the fury of his fighting but the composed Stevenson was not to be disturbed and the right hand continued to destroy the features of Bobick until he had an eye tightly closed and a side of his face puffed and distorted. And all the time Stevenson relentlessly shot in punches from his blind side and before the end of the second round it was clear that a million dollar dream was being shattered. The referee allowed the punishment to continue into the third round but not for long.

While the crowd talked of the magnificent Stevenson, Peter Hussing of West Germany toppled the Peruvian Ludena with a tremendous punch to set the locals ablaze. He was a magnificently built athlete and such was the punch that won him his fight in the first round that he could have been anything.

Stevenson quickly cut him down to size in the semi-final. He tolerated him for a minute until he had sized him up and then he found a gap between his squarely held hands and shot his right hand through. The punch hurt but the gap persisted and Stevenson settled down to throw mighty right-hand punches through the space and few missed the German chin. By the second round he was bloodied and bemused and in no fit state to continue. The contest was stopped.

In the other semi-final the Pole, Alexe, outpointed the Swede Thomsen and so was the next sacrificial victim for the feared Stevenson right hand. He was more fortunate than the others for he developed an arm injury and withdrew from the final to leave Stevenson with the gold medal.

Immediately there was speculation as to his future, but he insisted that he would continue to box as an amateur and hoped to win three Olympic gold medals. 'I don't believe in professionalism,' he said, 'I only believe in the revolution.' He returned to his studies at the University in Cuba.

For sure he will have to face considerable temptation, for his right hand seemed worth a million dollars of anybody's money and there were many around who would be prepared to chip in to take him from his native land, to places where such fighters are highly paid. He seemed firm enough in his resolve, but then he had to go home and face his president, Fidel Castro, who is much against professional boxing.

It would be a pleased Castro that Stevenson would face, for although Cuba had never previously won a gold medal, Cuban boxers won three of them in the Munich boxing. They were the most successful nation in a series which had been disastrous for the United States who won but one title and that with the composed light welter, Ray Seales.

Cuba's other winners were the bantamweight, Orlando Martinez, and the furious welterweight, Emilio Correa. Their wins were all the more meritorious in that the standards, although patchy, were generally agreed to be above those of Mexico.

Britain's representatives had pleased with controlled and well coached boxing and this was rewarded by three of them reaching the last eight. They took bronze medals and there was a big night for the British when the three went through for the medals within half an hour. Alan Minter at light-middle and George Turpin at bantam went through without the dissent of even one judge. Ralph Evans had a harder fight in beating the Ethiopian, Haile.

Minter from Crawley had fought with commendable aggression to overcome a muscular Algerian, Loucif Hanmani, to reach the last eight. The Algerian was a popular tip for the title. Minter overwhelmed with speed and skill and never allowed him to show the form that was previously so impressive.

Minter temporarily lost his composure mid-way through the fight when the referee warned him for making grunting noises as he punched. He had not known that this could be an offence and is still not convinced. The referee Abrahart classified it as intimidation. It was an untidy fight but always going Minter's way.

Minter had shocking luck in his next bout when he fought for a place in the semi-final. He met the West German Kottysch, a dour unimaginative fighter who predictably had the home crowd with him to a man. Against him Minter fought a wild, rash fight but he still did seem to have done enough to give him a clear win.

He had scrambled a bit in the second round and had an unusual warning for hitting with the inside of the glove, unusual, in that he does not slap and is generally agreed to be a good puncher. He piled on much pressure in the last round while the West German moved relentlessly forward but without doing damage. Minter and his party were confident that he had won and indeed there seemed to be few who did not.

When the judges' cards were revealed it was seen that two judges had voted for Minter and two for his opponent and the other had made them even but had given the advantage point to Kottysch. And so Minter was out and what irritated most was that when the final was fought and Kottysch beat the Pole Rudkowski—again on a split decision—the impression was that Minter would have beaten him even more easily and won a gold.

There were no such misgivings over the other British quarter finalists. Ralph Evans had boxed cleverly at light-fly but without a great deal of authority. He had given of his best in beating the Ethiopian, Haile, but in the semi-final he was out of his class against the experienced Hungarian, Gedo.

Gedo has been a top world performer for a long time. He is 23 and has been a member of the Hungarian national team since 1968 and was European Champion in 1971. Evans was not disgraced against him. Gedo won the final easily from the North Korean Kim.

George Turpin boxed as well as ever he had done in beating the good Kenyan, John Nderu. Turpin was at a disadvantage in height and reach, but he finished strongly to convince four of the five judges that he had won. Evans and Turpin had shared a room in the Olympic Village and they were overwhelmed at winning a medal each. They said, 'We came here to do our best but we never thought our best would win a medal.'

That was a sentiment which did not serve them well in the semi-final. Evans was well beaten but Turpin with a bit more enterprise would have won. He seemed to box as if he had no further ambition. He lost to the Cuban Martinez, but only by a split decision and one which could have gone either way.

Had he fought with as much determination as he did in the earlier rounds then he must have swayed at least one more judge and that would have given him the verdict. Again, there was the frustration that his conquerer Martinez went on to take the gold medal.

Nevertheless, the Great Britain coach, David James, had done extraordinarily well to have won three medals with what had been classed beforehand as indifferent material. It was a hopeful sign for British amateur boxing and confirmation that sensible coaching and training would pay off.

Eastern Europe did well with medals. The flyweight gold went to Gheorgi Kostadinov, a 21-year-old Bulgarian soldier, whose tip-and-run boxing took him easily through his fights. He was typical of the others from his part of the world.

Russia took a title with Boris Kousnetsov at featherweight, but it was not a popular verdict. There was an uproar when it was announced that he had beaten the veteran, Phillip Waruinge, of Kenya. He had been given a 3-2 split verdict. Waruinge, bronze medallist at the Mexico Olympics, did look to have beaten the 25-year-old Russian.

The lightweight title was clearly won by the 32-year-old European champion, Jan Szczepanski of Poland, who took an overwhelming verdict over the Hungarian, Orban. In a fight, between two of the most experienced boxers in the Games, Szczepanski used his left jab to dominate.

The sole United States finalist, light-welterweight Ray Seales, was a competent, composed fighter who fought his least impressive bout in the final but still beat the Bulgarian, Anghelov, although only on a split decision. Seales is a better fighter than he looked in the final in which he was carrying the whole hopes of the United States.

The quickest win was that of the Russian, Lemenchev, at middleweight. He took only two minutes to knock out the European bronze medallist Virtanen. The new champion is a 20-year-old soldier.

The Cubans already had three gold medals when their fourth finalist, Gilberto Carrillo, went into the ring. He had little chance against the European champion, Mate Parlov, and was knocked out 40 seconds before the end of the second round. At 19 years of age Carrillo is a fine prospect.

16

'A SORT OF SUBSTITUTE FOR WAR. . .?'

Monday, September 11th

These are the confessions of a middle-aged journalist who has been through too many emotional experiences during the past two weeks. He does not quite know whether his mind is tired through emotional stress, befuddled from lack of sleep, or whether he's arrived at the truth—which could well be a decadent truth. But I do know this: I hate fanaticism.

I hate fanatics who would deprive others of life because they are convinced that their cause is the right cause. I hate fanatics who will pursue one objective so relentlessly that they lose all sense of the completeness, the roundness of life.

And if you detect that I have already linked, and am about to do so again, the murder or suicide of seventeen people with what I have seen here in the Olympic stadia, then you are correct. If that seems obscene then you may be right, because I have seen so much obscenity this week that my senses may be blunted. Or you may be wrong, because I, being closer to the week's events than you, can detect their relationship.

We know what the fanaticism that grew up in the Munich beer cellars did to Europe and the world in the 1930's and 1940's. We know what Arab and Israeli fanaticism has done for the Middle East, the airlines of the world and now to some competitors in the Olympic Village. But are we quite certain that we know what fanaticism has done to sport? Let us take a few examples and then see whether there is anything worth preserving and, if there is, plan how to do it.

John Williams is a 19-year-old American whose sport is archery: images of Sherwood Forest, greensward, gallantry and Little John. It is no coincidence that Little John, a very big man, was a good archer. He was strong, and that is what an archer, ancient or modern, needs to be. So our modern Little John is given unlimited time by his employers—who happened to be the United States Army—and he trains six hours a day for seven days a week. With a little talent and an element of competitiveness in his make-up—and a drug, nicotine, to steady his nerves—it produces an Olympic gold medal. Ludicrous.

Or take a couple of examples nearer home: David Bedford and David Jenkins. I have an undying memory of Jenkins training this summer on the Meadowbank track in Edinburgh. The sun was behind him and he was pounding down the straight, his short blond hair juddering in the sunlight. It was an image of immense power and ferocity—really rather magnificent. Except that he did it time and time again and was on his knees, literally, crouched on the track, gasping for oxygen.

Yet this was an easy day's training. Those who saw him do a really hard session tell me that they saw him being physically sick. Do you wonder that on Monday he did not get into the final? He had left all his fire on that Meadowbank track.

A German athlete who runs 1500 metres in 3 min 39 sec (a good three seconds under four minutes for a mile) and is also a journalist, was sitting next to me in the Press seats when Jenkins ran his first heat last Sunday, and he said: 'He's going to have trouble.' And he did not mean trouble in reaching the final of the 400 metres. He meant trouble with his back. He told me the story of Gerhard Hennige, the German 400 metre hurdler who came between David Hemery and John Sherwood to win a silver medal in the Mexico Games.

Hennige, said this athlete, was the same sort of runner as Jenkins—not a floater, but a pounder, a man who used the bounce of an artificial track by hitting it as hard as he could with his feet. And now Hennige's back is giving him trouble because it has been subjected to too much vibration. Hennige is a physical education teacher as well as an athlete, and my German friend believes that he will have to change his profession because his back is too bad to carry on. There is no proof that Hennige's back trouble is connected with his running action on an artificial track. There is just the belief of his doctors that it is so. There is no proof or sign that the same thing will happen to Jenkins, and I hope passionately that it does not. But he is going to Montreal in four years' time and, because of his defeat here, he may well try to train still harder.

And then there is Bedford, who trains up to 200 miles a week—which is more than 28 miles every day—and others follow his example: like a runner called Roger Matthews from Bournemouth who had to go into hospital with kidney trouble because he was dehydrating his body every day.

There are limits, and I confess that I have been extremely slow in coming to this conclusion. And the reason for that is that people, especially journalists, have always talked about impossibilities—like the four-minute mile or climbing Everest—and yet others, the doers rather than the talkers, have refused to acknowledge these limits and were proved to be right. Besides, there is something magnificent about a man who refuses to acknowledge the impossible. Remember Browning's lines: 'Ah, but a man's reach should exceed his grasp, or what's a heaven for?'

So I wrestle with myself with one part of me standing back, as a good journalist should, and observing that it is all getting out of hand and fanatical. And the other part of me, that part that needs to become involved and test itself against the impossible barrier, saying that these are just the thoughts of a middle-aged man who has lost the fire in his belly.

I like, however, to think that I get wiser as I grow older and that my thoughts are more matured and based on experience. And I have what is known vulgarly as a 'gut reaction' which tells me that I should trust this maturity and reject the extremes. Which means that one must speak out and reject the whole concept of complete dedication to sport.

I was mulling these thoughts over with Hugh McIlvanney, once a colleague on *The Observer*, as we sat sipping a drink in the Press bar of the stadium. I pointed out that there was little difference that I could see between the dedication of the modern sportsman and that of of a classical pianist, or a ballet dancer, or a poet in a garret. He made the wise reply that the difference was that the pianist, for instance, did not just practise scales, but was being constantly subjected to the minds and emotions of the great composers. Of course he is right.

What distresses me is that utter fanaticism about the human body leads to utter neglect of the mind, and thus to a negation of that completeness of life that I mentioned earlier.

So what is to be done about it? First of all, we can change completely the showpiece of sport, the Olympic Games. We must stop them being a gladiatorial, nationalistic fight—a sort of a substitute for war between nations.

That means exorcising all nationalistic manifestations—the marching of the teams at the opening ceremony, the national anthems and the flags at the victory ceremony—and all sports and events in which there are national teams. It is easy to do. The closing ceremony, after all, in which the athletes come in higgledy–piggledy in a rejoicing mêlée, is far more moving than the formal, nationalistic opening ceremony. And a victory ceremony in which individuals are honoured with the Olympic anthem and the Olympic flag is far truer to the Olympic spirit than the present jingoistic affair. That, I can remember, is what I believed when I was a competitor in 1952 and 1956 and it is now an utter conviction.

Besides, it would ease the conscience of men like Wayne Collett, an intelligent American black man, who knew why he did not stand to attention when he was on the rostrum with the 400 metres winner, Vince Matthews, on Thursday. 'Because,' he said, 'I could not in all conscience respect what the flag stands for or the words of our national anthem when I know what my nation has done to my people.'

And by getting rid of all team sports (including the relays in athletics and swimming) you rid the games of more nationalism and help to reduce them to manageable proportions. But you have to go further than that and make it possible for hundreds of cities in the world to stage the Games instead of a handful. I reckon that means a maximum of about ten sports—very close to the nine sports of the Commonwealth Games (in which there are no team sports), a festival which is a delight to attend because of its unfrenetic atmosphere.

As I work it out, there are five sports which retain a permanent place: two represent speed on land and in the water (athletics and swimming); two represent individual combat (boxing and Judo, although I would hope that uncivilised boxing would eventually give way to civilised Judo); and one which represents skill allied with art (gymnastics). Then you allow another five sports on a rota basis—judging them on two criteria: that they are universal and recreational.

Finally, you hold these Games every two years so that a young man does not have to devote such a long period of his youth to preparation and so that you do not have sporting tragedies like that of Jim Ryun or Ron Clarke, both of them acknowledged by their fellow athletes to be the greatest in their respective events, although neither has the visible proof and personal satisfaction of an Olympic gold medal.

Of course, it will not solve all the problems of the Olympics or of sport. But who could do that? All one can do is to trust human nature and instinct (provided you believe that man is basically good rather than basically evil). It seems to me that there is a current running through the human spirit which is rejecting extremes whether they be the fanatical pursuit of money, the fanatical pursuit of glory or the fanatical pursuit of a cause.

I do know this, with certainty: something drastic must be done before the Games open in four years' time in Montreal—a city which has also known the problem of hostages and which has seen, very recently, the senseless destruction of human life.

THE BRITISH MEDAL WINNERS

GOLD

Mary Peters	(Pentathlon)
Richard Meade	(Individual Three-Day Event)
Richard Meade Mary Gordon-Watson Bridget Parker Mark Phillips	(Three-Day Event)
Rodney Pattisson Chris Davies	(Yachting—Flying Dutchman)

SILVER

Ann Moore	(Individual Show Jumping)
Martin Reynolds Alan Pascoe David Hemery David Jenkins	(4 × 400 metres Relay)
David Starbrook	(Judo—Middle-Heavyweight)
David Wilkie	(200 metres Breaststroke)
Alan Warren David Hunt	(Yachting—Tempest)

BRONZE

David Hemery	(400 metres Hurdles)
Ian Stewart	(5000 Metres)
Ralph Evans	(Boxing—Light-Flyweight)
George Turpin	(Boxing—Bantamweight)
Alan Minter	(Boxing—Light-Middleweight)
Mick Bennett Ian Hallam Ronald Keeble Willie Moore	(Cycling—Team Pursuit)
Brian Jacks	(Judo—Middleweight)
Alan Parisi	(Judo—Open)
John Kynoch	(Shooting—Moving Target)

MUNICH 72—*RESULTS*

MEN'S ATHLETICS

Track Events

100 METRES

1. V. Borzov (U.S.S.R.)	10.14 sec
2. R. Taylor (U.S.A.)	10.24 sec
3. L. Miller (Jamaica)	10.33 sec
4. A. Kornelyuk (U.S.S.R.)	10.36 sec
5. M. Fray (Jamaica)	10.40 sec
6. J. Hirscht (West Germany)	10.40 sec
7. Z. Nowosz (Poland)	10.46 sec
(H. Crawford (Trinidad) retired)	

400 METRES

1. V. Matthews (U.S.A.)	44.66 sec
2. W. Collett (U.S.A.)	44.80 sec
3. J. Sang (Kenya)	44.92 sec
4. C. Asati (Kenya)	45.13 sec
5. H. Schloeske (West Germany)	45.31 sec
6. M. Kukkoaho (Finland)	45.49 sec
7. K. Honz (West Germany	45.68 sec
(J. Smith (U.S.A.) retired)	

1500 METRES

1. P. Vasala (Finland)	3 min 36.3 sec
2. K. Keino (Kenya)	3 min 36.8 sec
3. R. Dixon (New Zealand)	3 min 37.5 sec
4. M. Boit (Kenya)	3 min 38.4 sec
5. B. Foster (G.B.)	3 min 39.0 sec
6. H. Mignon (Belgium)	3 min 39.1 sec
7. P.-H. Wellmann (West Germany)	3 min 40.1 sec
8. V. Pantelei (U.S.S.R.)	3 min 40.2 sec
9. A. Polhill (New Zealand)	3 min 41.8 sec
10. T. Hansen (Denmark)	3 min 46.6 sec

10,000 METRES

1. L. Viren (Finland)	27 min 38.4 sec
(World and Olympic record)	
2. E. Puttemans (Belgium)	23 min 39.6 sec
3. M. Yifter (Ethiopia)	27 min 41.0 sec
4. M. Haro (Spain)	27 min 48.2 sec
5. F. Shorter (U.S.A.)	27 min 51.4 sec
6. D. Bedford (G.B.)	28 min 05.4 sec
7. D. Korica (Yugoslavia)	28 min 15.2 sec
8. A. Zaddem (Tunisia)	28 min 18.2 sec

200 METRES

1. V. Borzov (U.S.S.R.)	20.00 sec
2. L. Black (U.S.A.)	20.19 sec
3. P. Mennea (Italy)	20.30 sec
4. L. Burton (U.S.A.)	20.37 sec
5. C. Smith (U.S.A.)	20.55 sec
6. S. Schenke (East Germany)	20.56 sec
7. M. Icllinghaus (West Germany)	20.65 sec
8. H.-J. Zenk (East Germany)	21.05 sec

800 METRES

1. D. Wottle (U.S.A.)	1 min 45.9 sec
2. B. Arzhanov (U.S.S.R.)	1 min 45.9 sec
3. M. Boit (Kenya)	1 min 46.0 sec
4. F. J. Kemper (West Germany)	1 min 46.5 sec
5. R. Ouko (Kenya)	1 min 46.5 sec
6. A. Carter (G.B.)	1 min 46.6 sec
7. A. Kupczyk (Poland)	1 min 47.1 sec
8. D. Fromm (East Germany)	1 min 48.0 sec

5000 METRES

1. L. Viren (Finland)	13 min 26.4 sec
(Olympic record)	
2. M. Gammoudi (Tunisia)	13 min 27.4 sec
3. I. Stewart (G.B.)	13 min 27.6 sec
4. S. Prefontaine (U.S.A.)	13 min 28.4 sec
5. E. Puttemans (Belgium)	13 min 30.8 sec
6. H. Norpoth (West Germany)	13 min 32.6 sec
7. P. Halle (Norway)	13 min 34.4 sec
8. N. Sviridov (U.S.S.R.)	13 min 39.4 sec
9. F. Eisenberg (East Germany)	13 min 40.8 sec
10. J. Alvarez (Spain)	13 min 41.8 sec
11. I. McCafferty (G.B.)	13 min 43.2 sec
12. D. Bedford (G.B.)	13 min 43.2 sec
13. J. Vaatainen (Finland)	13 min 53.8 sec

MARATHON

1. F. Shorter (U.S.A.)	2 hr 12 min 19.8 sec
2. K. Lismont (Belgium)	2 hr 14 min 31.8 sec
3. M. Wolde (Ethiopia)	2 hr 15 min 08.4 sec
4. K. Moore (U.S.A.)	2 hr 15 min 39.8 sec
5. K. Kimihara (Japan)	2 hr 16 min 27.0 sec
6. R. Hill (G.B.)	2 hr 16 min 30.6 sec
7. D. MacGregor (G.B.)	2 hr 16 min 34.4 sec
8. J. Foster (New Zealand)	2 hr 16 min 56.2 sec
9. J. Bacheler (U.S.A.)	2 hr 17 min 38.2 sec
10. L. Bedane (Ethiopia)	2 hr 18 min 36.8 sec
20. C. Kirkham (G.B.)	2 hr 21 min 54.8 sec

3000 METRES STEEPLECHASE

1.	K. Keino (Kenya) (Olympic record)	8 min 23.6 sec
2.	B. Jipcho (Kenya)	8 min 24.6 sec
3.	T. Kantanen (Finland)	8 min 24.8 sec
4.	B. Malinowski (Poland)	8 min 28.0 sec
5.	D. Moravcik (Czechoslovakia)	8 min 29.2 sec
6.	A. Biwott (Kenya)	8 min 33.6 sec
7.	R. Bitte (U.S.S.R.)	8 min 34.6 sec
8.	P. Paeivaerinta (Finland)	8 min 37.2 sec
9.	T. Koyams (Japan)	8 min 37.8 sec

400 METRES HURDLES

1.	J. Akii-Bua (Uganda) (World and Olympic record)	47.82 sec
2.	R. Mann (U.S.A.)	48.51 sec
3.	D. Hemery (G.B.)	48.52 sec
4.	J. Seymour (U.S.A.)	48.64 sec
5.	R. Schubert (West Germany)	49.65 sec
6.	E. Gavrilenko (U.S.S.R.)	49.66 sec
7.	S. Tziortzis (Greece)	49.66 sec
8.	Y. Zorin (U.S.S.R.)	50.25 sec

110 METRES HURDLES

1.	R. Milburn (U.S.A.)	13.24 sec
2.	G. Drut (France)	13.34 sec
3.	T. Hill (U.S.A.)	13.48 sec
4.	W. Davenport (U.S.A.)	13.50 sec
5.	F. Siebeck (East Germany)	13.71 sec
6.	L. Wodzynski (Poland)	13.72 sec
7.	L. Nadenicek (Czechoslovakia)	13.76 sec
8.	P. Cech (Czechoslovakia)	13.86 sec

4 × 100 METRES RELAY

1.	U.S.A. (equals World and Olympic record)	38.19 sec
2.	Russia	38.50 sec
3.	West Germany	38.79 sec
4.	Czechoslovakia	38.82 sec
5.	East Germany	38.90 sec
6.	Poland	39.03 sec
7.	France	39.14 sec
8.	Italy	39.14 sec

4 × 400 METRES RELAY

1.	Kenya	2 min 59.8 sec
2.	G.B. (M. Reynolds, A. Pascoe, D. Hemery, D. Jenkins)	3 min 00.5 sec
3.	France	3 min 00.7 sec
4.	West Germany	3 min 00.9 sec
5.	Poland	3 min 01.1 sec
6.	Finland	3 min 01.1 sec
7.	Sweden	3 min 02.6 sec
8.	Trinidad and Tobago	3 min 03.6 sec

Field Events

HIGH JUMP

1.	Y. Tarmak (U.S.S.R.)	7 ft 3¾ in
2.	S. Junge (East Germany)	7 ft 3 in
3.	D. Stones (U.S.A.)	7 ft 3 in
4.	H. Magerl (West Germany)	7 ft 1¾ in
5.	A. Szepesi (Holland)	7 ft 1¾ in
6.	I. Major (Holland)	7 ft 0¾ in
	J. Beers (Canada)	7 ft 0¾ in
8.	R. Akhmetov (U.S.S.R.)	7 ft 0¾ in
9.	J. Hawkins (Canada)	7 ft 0¾ in
10.	E. del Forno (Italy)	7 ft 0¾ in

POLE VAULT

1.	W. Nordwig (East Germany) (Olympic record)	18 ft 0½ in
2.	R. Seagren (U.S.A.)	17 ft 8½ in
3.	J. Johnson (U.S.A.)	16 ft 6¾ in
4.	R. Kuretzky (West Germany)	17 ft 4¾ in
5.	R. Simpson (Canada)	17 ft 0¾ in
6.	V. Ohl (West Germany)	17 ft 0¾ in
7.	H. Lagerqvist (Spain)	17 ft 0¾ in
8.	F. Trancanelli (France)	16 ft 8¾ in

LONG JUMP

1. R. Williams (U.S.A.)	27 ft 0½ in
2. H. Baumgartner (West Germany)	26 ft 10 in
3. A. Robinson (U.S.A.)	26 ft 4¼ in
4. J. Owusu (Ghana)	26 ft 3½ in
5. P. Carrington (U.S.A.)	26 ft 2½ in
6. M. Klauss (East Germany)	26 ft 1½ in
7. A. Lerwill (G.B.)	25 ft 11½ in
8. E. Barkovski (U.S.S.R.)	25 ft 5¼ in

SHOT-PUT

1. W. Komar (Poland)	69 ft 6 in
2. G. Woods (U.S.A.)	69 ft 5½ in
3. H. Briesenick (East Germany)	69 ft 4¾ in
4. H.-P. Gies (East Germany)	69 ft 4¼ in
5. A. Fuerbach (U.S.A.)	68 ft 11¼ in
6. B. Oldfield (U.S.A.)	68 ft 7¼ in
7. H. Birlenbach (West Germany)	66 ft 10 in
8. V. Varju (Holland)	65 ft 11¼ in

HAMMER-THROW

1. A. Bondarchuk (U.S.S.R.) (Olympic record)	247 ft 8½ in
2. J. Sachse (East Germany)	245 ft 11 in
3. V. Khmelevski (U.S.S.R.)	242 ft 11 in
4. U. Beyer (West Germany)	234 ft 7¾ in
5. G. Zsivotsky (Holland)	234 ft 2¾ in
6. S. Eckschmiedt (Holland)	233 ft 7 in
7. E. Klein (West Germany)	233 ft 4¾ in
8. S. Murofushi (Japan)	232 ft 6½ in
16. B. Williams (G.B.)	223 ft 8¼ in

20 KILOMETRES WALK

1. P. Frenkel (East Germany) (Olympic record)	1 hr 26 min 42.4 sec
2. V. Golubnichi (U.S.S.R.)	1 hr 26 min 55.2 sec
3. H. Reimann (East Germany)	1 hr 27 min 16.6 sec
4. G. Sperling (East Germany)	1 hr 27 min 55.0 sec
5. N. Smaga (U.S.S.R.)	1 hr 28 min 16.6 sec
6. P. Nihill (G.B.)	1 hr 28 min 44.4 sec
7. V. Ornoch (Poland)	1 hr 32 min 01.6 sec
8. V. Visini (Italy)	1 hr 32 min 30.6 sec
14. P. Embleton (G.B.)	1 hr 33 min 22.2 sec
17. P. Marlow (G.B.)	1 hr 35 min 38.8 sec

DECATHLON

1. N. Avilov (U.S.S.R.) (World and Olympic record)	8454 pts
2. L. Litvinenko (U.S.S.R.)	8035 pts
3. R. Katus (Poland)	7984 pts
4. J. Bennett (U.S.A.)	7974 pts
5. S. Schreyer (East Germany)	7950 pts
6. F. Herbrand (Belgium)	7947 pts
7. S. Jensen (Denmark)	7947 pts
8. T. Janczenko (Poland)	7861 pts
15. B. King (G.B.)	7468 pts
(P. Gabbett (G.B.) retired)	

TRIPLE JUMP

1. V. Saneyev (U.S.S.R.)	56 ft 11 in
2. J. Drehmel (East Germany)	56 ft 9½ in
3. N. Prudencio (Brazil)	55 ft 11¼ in
4. C. Corbu (Rumania)	55 ft 3½ in
5. J. Craft (U.S.A.)	55 ft 2½ in
6. M. Dia (Senegal)	55 ft 2½ in
7. M. Joachimowski (Poland)	54 ft 9 in
8. K. Floegstad (Norway)	53 ft 11¼ in

DISCUS

1. L. Danek (Czechoslovakia)	211 ft 3½ in
2. J. Silvester (U.S.A.)	208 ft 8 in
3. R. Bruch (Spain)	208 ft
4. J. Powell (U.S.A.)	206 ft 1¼ in
5. G. Fejer (Holland)	205 ft 5½ in
6. E. Thorith (East Germany)	204 ft 9½ in
7. F. Tegla (Holland)	198 ft 9¾ in
8. T. Vollmer (U.S.A.)	197 ft 7½ in

JAVELIN

1. K. Wolfermann (West Germany) (Olympic record)	296 ft 10 in
2. J. Lusis (U.S.S.R.)	296 ft 9½ in
3. W. Schmidt (U.S.A.)	276 ft 11½ in
4. H. Siitonen (Finland)	276 ft 7½ in
5. B. Grimnes (Norway)	272 ft 7 in
6. J. Kinnunen (Finland)	269 ft 3½ in
7. M. Nemeth (Holland)	268 ft 11½ in
8. F. Luke (U.S.A.)	262 ft 8 in

50 KILOMETRES WALK

1. B. Kannenberg (West Germany) (Olympic Record)	3 hr 56 min 11.6 sec
2. V. Soldatenko (U.S.S.R.)	3 hr 58 min 24.0 sec
3. L. Young (U.S.A.	4 hr 00 min 46.0 sec
4. O. Barch (U.S.S.R.)	4 hr 01 min 35.4 sec
5. P. Selzer (East Germany)	4 hr 04 min 05.4 sec
6. G. Weidner (West Germany)	4 hr 06 min 26.0 sec
7. V. Visini (Italy)	4 hr 08 min 31.4 sec
8. G. Hernandez (Mexico)	4 hr 12 min 09.0 sec
9. P. Nihill (G.B.)	4 hr 14 min 09.4 sec
18. J. Warhurst (G.B.)	4 hr 23 min 21.6 sec
25. H. Timms (G.B.)	4 hr 34 min 43.8 sec

MODERN PENTATHLON

Individual result

1. A. Balczo (Holland)	5412 pts
2. Onischenko (U.S.S.R.)	5335 pts
3. P. Lednev (U.S.S.R.)	5328 pts
4. J. Fox (G.B.)	5311 pts
5. V. Shmelev (U.S.S.R.)	5302 pts
6. B. Ferm (Spain)	5283 pts
7. H. Thade (West Germany)	5145 pts
8. R. Hurme (Finland)	5094 pts
9. C. Richards (U.S.A.)	5074 pts
10. M. Gueguen (France)	5072 pts
36. B. Lillywhite (G.B.)	4527 pts
47. R. Phelps (G.B.)	4385 pts

MODERN PENTATHLON (*cont.*)

Team result

1. U.S.S.R.	15,968 pts
2. Hungary	15,348 pts
3. Finland	14,812 pts
4. U.S.A.	14,802 pts
5. Sweden	14,708 pts
6. West Germany	14,682 pts
7. France	14,559 pts
8. Poland	14,258 pts
9. G.B.	14,257 pts
10. Italy	13,913 pts

WOMEN'S ATHLETICS

Track Events

100 METRES

1. R. Stecher (East Germany)	11.07 sec
2. R. Boyle (Australia)	11.23 sec
3. S. Chivas (Cuba)	11.24 sec
4. I. Davis (U.S.A.)	11.32 sec
5. A. Richter (East Germany)	11.38 sec
6. A. Annum (Ghana)	11.41 sec
7. B. Ferrell (U.S.A.)	11.45 sec
8. E. Gleskova (Czechoslovakia)	12.48 sec

400 METRES

1. M. Zehrt (East Germany) (Olympic record)	51.08 sec
2. R. Wilden (West Germany)	51.21 sec
3. K. Hammond (U.S.A.)	51.64 sec
4. H. Seidler (East Germany)	51.86 sec
5. M. Fergerson (U.S.A.)	51.96 sec
6. C. Rendina (Australia)	51.99 sec
7. D. Kaesling (East Germany)	52.19 sec
8. G. Balogh (Holland)	52.39 sec

1500 METRES

1. L. Bragina (U.S.S.R.) (World and Olympic record)	4 min 01.4 sec
2. G. Hoffmeister (East Germany)	4 min 02.8 sec
3. P. Cacchi (Italy)	4 min 02.9 sec
4. K. Burneleit (East Germany)	4 min 04.1 sec
5. S. Carey (G.B.)	4 min 04.8 sec
6. I. Keizer (Netherlands)	4 min 05.1 sec
7. T. Pangelova (U.S.S.R.)	4 min 06.5 sec
8. J. Orr (Australia)	4 min 12.2 sec
9. B. Boxem (Netherlands)	4 min 13.1 sec
(E. Tittel (West Germany) retired)	

4 × 100 METRES RELAY

1. West Germany (equals World and Olympic records)	42.81 sec
2. East Germany	42.95 sec
3. Cuba	43.36 sec
4. U.S.A.	43.39 sec
5. U.S.S.R.	43.59 sec
6. Australia	43.61 sec
7. G.B.	43.71 sec
8. Poland	44.20 sec

200 METRES

1. R. Stecher (East Germany) (equals World record)	22.40 sec
2. R. Boyle (Australia)	22.45 sec
3. I. Szewinska (Poland)	22.74 sec
4. E. Strophal (East Germany)	22.75 sec
5. A. Kroniger (West Germany)	22.89 sec
C. Heinich (East Germany)	22.89 sec
7. A. Annum (Ghana)	22.99 sec
8. R. Allwood (Jamaica)	23.11 sec

800 METRES

1. H. Falck (West Germany) (Olympic record)	1 min 58.6 sec
2. N. Sabaite (U.S.S.R.)	1 min 58.7 sec
3. G. Hoffmeister (East Germany)	1 min 59.2 sec
4. S. Zlateva (Bulgaria)	1 min 59.7 sec
5. V. Nikolic (Yugoslavia)	2 min 00.0 sec
6. I. Silai (Rumania)	2 min 00.0 sec
7. R. Stirling G.B.)	2 min 00.2 sec
8. A. Hoffman (Canada)	2 min 00.2 sec

100 METRES HURDLES

1. A. Ehrhardt (East Germany) (Olympic record)	12.59 sec
2. V. Bufanu (Rumania)	12.84 sec
3. K. Balzer (East Germany)	12.90 sec
4. P. Ryan (Australia)	12.98 sec
5. T. Nowak (Poland)	13.17 sec
6. D. Straszynska (Poland)	13.18 sec
7. A. Krumpholz (East Germany)	13.27 sec
8. G. Rabsztyn (Poland)	13.44 sec

4 × 400 METRES RELAY

1. East Germany (World and Olympic record)	3 min 23.0 sec
2. United States	3 min 25.2 sec
3. West Germany	3 min 26.5 sec
4. France	3 min 27.5 sec
5. G.B.	3 min 28.7 sec
6. Australia	3 min 28.8 sec
7. Finland	3 min 29.4 sec
8. U.S.S.R.	3 min 31.9 sec

Field Events

HIGH JUMP

1. U. Meyfarth (West Germany) (equal World and Olympic record)	6 ft 3½ in
2. Y. Blagoeva (Bulgaria)	6 ft 2 in
3. I. Gusenbauer (Austria)	6 ft 2 in
4. P. Inkpen (G.B.)	6 ft 0¾ in
5. R. Schmidt (East Germany)	6 ft 0¾ in
6. S. Simeoni (Italy)	6 ft 0¾ in
7. R. Witschas (East Germany)	6 ft 0¾ in
8. D. Brill (Canda)	5 ft 11¾ in

SHOT

1. N. Chizhova (U.S.S.R. (World and Olympic record)	69 ft 0 in
2. M. Gummel (East Germany)	66 ft 4 in
3. I. Khristova (Bulgaria)	63 ft 5¾ in
4. E. Dolzhenko (U.S.S.R.)	63 ft 1½ in
5. M. Adam (East Germany)	62 ft 1¾ in
6. M. Lange (East Germany)	61 ft 10¼ in
7. H. Fibingerova (Czechoslovakia)	61 ft 8½ in
8. E. Stoyanova (Bulgaria)	60 ft 2 in

JAVELIN

1. R. Fuchs (East Germany) (Olympic record)	209 ft 7 in
2. J. Todten (East Germany)	205 ft 2 in
3. K. Schmidt (U.S.A.)	196 ft 8 in
4. L. Mollova (Bulgaria)	194 ft 9 in
5. N. Urbancic (Yugoslavia)	193 ft 9 in
6. E. Janko (Austria)	192 ft 1½ in
7. E. Gryziecka (Poland)	187 ft 0 in
8. S. Koroliova (U.S.S.R.)	184 ft 11 in

LONG JUMP

1. H. Rosendahl (West Germany)	22 ft 3 in
2. D. Yorgova (Bulgaria)	22 ft 2½ in
3. E. Suranova (Czechoslovakia)	22 ft 1½ in
4. M. Garbey (Cuba)	21 ft 4¾ in
5. H. Schueller (West Germany)	21 ft 4¼ in
6. M. Antenen (Switzerland)	21ft 3½ in
7. V. Viscopoleanu (Rumania)	21 ft 3¼ in
8. M. Olfert (East Germany)	21 ft 2¼ in
9. S. Sherwood (G.B.)	21 ft 0¼ in

DISCUS

1. F. Melnik (U.S.S.R.) (Olympic record)	218 ft 7 in
2. A. Menis (Rumania)	213 ft 5½ in
3. V. Stoeva (Bulgaria)	211 ft 1 in
4. T. Danilova (U.S.S.R.)	206 ft 2¾ in
5. L. Westermann (West Germany)	204 ft 0 in
6. G. Hinzmann (East Germany)	202 ft 6 in
12. R. Payne (G.B.)	185 ft 4 in

PENTATHLON

1. M. Peters (G.B.) (World and Olympic record)	4801 pts
2. H. Rosendahl (West Germany)	4791 pts
3. B. Pollak (East Germany)	4768 pts
4. C. Bodner (East Germany)	4671 pts
5. V. Tikhomirova (U.S.S.R.)	4597 pts
6. N. Anghelova (Bulgaria)	4496 pts
7. K. Mack (West Germany)	4449 pts
8. I. Bruzsenyak (Hungary)	4419 pts
13. A. Wilson (G.B.)	4279 pts

SWIMMING

Men

100 METRES FREE-STYLE

1. M. Spitz (U.S.A.) (World and Olympic record)	51.22 sec
2. J. Heidenreich (U.S.A.)	51.65 sec
3. V. Bure (U.S.S.R.)	51.77 sec
4. J. Murphy (U.S.A.)	52.08 sec
5. M. Wenden (Australia)	52.41 sec
6. I. Grivennikov (U.S.S.R.)	52.44 sec
7. M. Rousseau (France)	52.90 sec
8. K. Steinbach (West Germany)	52.92 sec

400 METRES FREE-STYLE

1. R. Demont (U.S.A.) (Olympic record)	4 min 00.26 sec
2. B. Cooper (Australia)	4 min 00.27 sec
3. S. Genter (U.S.A.)	4 min 01.94 sec
4. T. McBreen (U.S.A.)	4 min 02.64 sec
5. G. Windeatt (Austrlia)	4 min 02.93 sec
6. B. Brinkley (G.B.)	4 min 06.69 sec
7. B. Gingsjoe (Sweden)	4 min 06.75 sec
8. W. Lampe (West Germany	4 min 06.97 sec

Note: Rick Demont (U.S.A.) who came first in the 400 Metres Freestyle was disqualified for taking a banned drug. The I.O.C. awarded his Gold medal to Brad Cooper. Cooper's Silver was awarded to Steve Genter.

200 METRES FREE-STYLE

1. M. Spitz (U.S.A.) (World and Olympic record)	1 min 52.78 sec
2. S. Genter (U.S.A.)	1 min 53.73 sec
3. W. Lampke (West Germany)	1 min 53.99 sec
4. M. Wenden (Austrlia)	1 min 54.40 sec
5. F. Tyler (U.S.A.)	1 min 54.96 sec
6. K. Steinbach (West Germany)	1 min 55.65 sec
3. V. Bure (U.S.S.R.)	1 min 57.24 sec
8. R. Hutton (Canada)	1 min 57.56 sec

1500 METRES FREE-STYLE

1. M. Burton (U.S.A.) (World and Olympic record)	15 min 52.58 sec
2. G. Windeatt (Australia)	15 min 58.48 sec
3. D. Northway (U.S.A.)	16 min 09.25 sec
4. B. Gingsjoe (Sweden)	16 min 16.01 sec
5. G. White (Australia)	16 min 17.22 sec
6. M. Treffers (New Zealand)	16 min 18.24 sec
7. B. Cooper (Australia)	16 min 30.49 sec
8. G. Garcia (Mexico)	16 min 36.03 sec

100 METRES BREASTSTROKE

1. N. Taguchi (Japan) (World and Olympic record)	1 min 04.94 sec
2. T. Bruce (U.S.A.)	1 min 05.43 sec
3. J. Hencken (U.S.A.)	1 min 05.61 sec
4. M. Chatfield (U.S.A.)	1 min 06.01 sec
5. W. Kusch (West Germany)	1 min 06.23 sec
6. J. Fiolo (Brazil)	1 min 06.24 sec
7. N. Pankin (U.S.S.R.)	1 min 06.36 sec
8. D. Wilkie (G.B.)	1 min 06.52 sec

100 METRES BUTTERFLY

1. M. Spitz (U.S.A.) (World and Olympic record)	54.27 sec
2. B. Robertson (Canada)	55.56 sec
3. J. Heidenreich (U.S.A.)	55.74 sec
4. R. Matthes (East Germany)	55.87 sec
5. D. Edgar (U.S.A.)	56.11 sec
6. B. MacDonald (Canada)	57.27 sec
7. H. Floeckner (East Germany)	57.40 sec
8. N. Robers (Australia)	57.90 sec

100 METRES BACKSTROKE

1. R. Matthes (East Germany) (Olympic record)	56.58 sec
2. M. Stamm (U.S.A.)	57.70 sec
3. J. Murphy (U.S.A.)	58.35 sec
4. M. Ivey (U.S.A.)	58.48 sec
5. L. Grivennikov (U.S.S.R.)	59.50 sec
6. L. Wanja (East Germany)	59.80 sec
7. J. Krueger (East Germany)	59.93 sec
8. T. Honda (Japan)	1 min 00.41 sec

200 METRES INDIVIDUAL MEDLEY

1. G. Larsson (Sweden) (World and Olympic record)	2 min 07.17 sec
2. T. McKee (U.S.A.)	2 min 08.37 sec
3. S. Furniss (U.S.A.)	2 min 08.45 sec
4. G. Hall (U.S.A.)	2 min 08.49 sec
5. A. Hargitay (Hungary)	2 min 09.66 sec
6. M. Suharev (U.S.S.R.)	2 min 11.78 sec
7. J. Bello (Peru)	2 min 11.87 sec
8. H. Ljunberg (Sweden)	2 min 13.56 sec

4×100 METRES FREE-STYLE RELAY

1. U.S.A. (World and Olympic record)	3 min 26.42 sec
2. U.S.S.R.	3 min 29.73 sec
3. East Germany	3 min 32.42 sec
4. Brazil	3 min 33.14 sec
5. Canada	3 min 33.2 sec
6. West Germany	3 min 33.9 sec
7. France	3 min 34.13 sec
8. Spain	3 min 38.21 sec

4×100 METRES MEDLEY RELAY

1. U.S.A. (World and Olympic record)	3 min 48.16 sec
2. East Germany	3 min 52.1 sec
3. Canada	3 min 52.26 sec
4. U.S.S.R.	3 min 53.26 sec
5. Brazil	3 min 57.89 sec
6. Japan	3 min 58.23 sec
7. G.B.	3 min 58.82 sec
8. Hungary	3 min 59.07 sec

200 METRES BREASTSTROKE

1. J. Hencken (U.S.A.) (World and Olympic record)	2 min 21.55 se
2. D. Wilkie (G.B.)	2 min 23.67 sec
3. N. Taguchi (Japan)	2 min 23.88 sec
4. R. Colella (U.S.A.)	2 min 24.28 sec
5. F. Munoz (Mexico)	2 min 26.44 sec
6. W. Kusch (West Germany)	2 min 26.55 sec
7. I. Cherdakov (U.S.S.R.)	2 min 27.15 sec
8. K. Katzur (East Germany)	2 min 27.44 sec

200 METRES BUTTERFLY

1. M. Spitz (U.S.A.) (World and Olympic record)	2 min 00.70 sec
2. G. Hall (U.S.A.)	2 min 02.86 sec
3. R. Backhaus (U.S.A.)	2 min 03.23 sec
4. J. Delgado (Ecuador)	2 min 04.60 sec
5. H. Fassnacht (West Germany)	2 min 04.69 sec
A. Hargitay (Hungary)	2 min 04.69 sec
7. H. Fleckner (East Germany)	2 min 05.34 sec
8. F. Meeuw (West Germany)	2 min 05.57 sec

200 METRES BACKSTROKE

1. R. Matthes (East Germany) (equals World record)	2 min 02.82 sec
2. M. Stamm (U.S.A.)	2 min 04.09 sec
3. M. Ivey (U.S.A.)	2 min 04.33 sec
4. B. Cooper (Australia)	2 min 06.59 sec
5. T. McKee (U.S.A.)	2 min 07.29 sec
6. L. Noack (East Germany)	2 min 08.67 sec
7. Z. Verraszto (Hungary)	2 min 10.09 sec
8. J.-P. Berjeaud (France)	2 min 11.77 sec

400 METRES INDIVIDUAL MEDLEY

1. G. Larsson (Sweden) (Olympic record)	4 min 31.981 sec
2. T. McKee (U.S.A.)	4 min 31.983 sec
3. A. Hargitay (Hungary)	4 min 32.70 sec
4. S. Furniss (U.S.A.)	4 min 35.44 sec
5. G. Hall (U.S.A.)	4 min 37.38 sec
6. B. Gingsjoe (Sweden)	4 min 37.96 sec
7. G. Windeatt (Australia)	4 min 40.39 sec
8. W. Sperling (East Germany)	4 min 40.66 sec

4×200 METRES FREE-STYLE RELAY

1. U.S.A. (World and Olympic record)	7 min 35.78 sec
2. West Germany	7 min 41.69 sec
3. U.S.S.R.	7 min 45.76 sec
4. Sweden	7 min 47.37 sec
5. Australia	7 min 48.66 sec
6. East Germany	7 min 49.11 sec
7. Canada	7 min 53.61 sec
8. G.B.	7 min 55.59 sec

HIGHBOARD DIVING

1. K. Dibiasi (Italy)	504.12 pts
2. R. Rydze (U.S.A.)	480.75 pts
3. F. Clagnotto (Italy)	475.83 pts
4. L. Matthes (East Germany)	465.75 pts
5. D. Ambarcumian (U.S.S.R.)	463.56 pts
6. R. Early (U.S.A.)	462.45 pts
7. V. Kapirulin (U.S.S.R.)	459.21 pts
8. C. Giron (Mexico)	442.41 pts
9. M. Finneran (U.S.A.)	439.47 spt
10. F. Hoffman (East Germany)	436.71 pts
11. D. Wagstaff (Australia)	435.84 pts
12. A. Gendrikson (U.S.S.R.)	431.04 pts

SPRINGBOARD DIVING

1. V. Vasin (U.S.S.R.)	594.09 pts
2. F. Cagnotto (Italy)	591.63 pts
3. C. Lincoln (U.S.A.)	577.29 pts
4. K. Dibiasi (Italy)	559.05 pts
5. M. Finneran (U.S.A.)	577.34 pts
6. V. Strabov (U.S.S.R.)	556.20 pts
7. E. Hoffman (East Germany)	544.95 pts
8. N. Huda (West Germany)	524.16 pts
9. C. Giron (Mexico)	521.88 pts
10. R. Loken (Norway)	514.92 pts
11. J. Robinson (Mexico)	514.02 pts
12. H. Ziethen (East Germany)	511.02 pts

SWIMMING

Women

100 METRES FREE-STYLE

1. S. Neilson (U.S.A.) (Olympic record)	58.59 sec
2. S. Babashoff (U.S.A.)	59.02 sec
3. S. Gould (Australia)	59.06 sec
4. G. Wetzko (East Germany)	59.21 sec
5. H. Reineck (West Germany)	59.73 sec
6. A. Eife (East Germany)	59.91 sec
7. M. Patoh (Hungary)	1 min 00.02 sec
8. E. Brigitha (Netherlands)	1 min 00.09 sec

400 METRES FREE-STYLE

1. S. Gould (Australia) (World and Olympic record)	4 min 19.04 sec
2. N. Calligaris (Italy)	4 min 24.44 sec
3. G. Wegner (East Germany)	4 min 23.11 sec
4. S. Babashoff (U.S.A.)	4 min 23.59 sec
5. J. Wylie (U.S.A.)	4 min 24.07 sec
6. K. Rothammer (U.S.A.)	4 min 24.22 sec
7. H. Bunschoten (Netherlands)	4 min 29.70 sec
8. A. Ridjners (Netherlands)	4 min 31.51 sec

100 METRES BREASTSTROKE

1. C. Carr (U.S.A.) (World and Olympic record)	1 min 13.58 sec
2. G. Stepanova (U.S.S.R.)	1 min 14.99 sec
3. B. Whitfield (Australia)	1 min 15.73 sec
4. A. Kissne-Kaczander (Hungary)	1 min 16.26 sec
5. J. Melick (U.S.A.)	1 min 16.34 sec
6. V. Eberle (West Germany)	1 min 17.16 sec
7. B.-M. Smedh (Sweden)	1 min 17.19 sec
8. D. Harrison (G.B.)	1 min 17.49 sec

100 METRES BUTTERFLY

1. M. Oaki (Japan) (World and Olympic record)	1 min 03.34 sec
2. R. Beier (East Germany)	1 min 03.61 sec
3. A. Gyarmati (Hungary)	1 min 03.73 sec
4. D. Deardurff (U.S.A.)	1 min 03.95 sec
5. D. Shrader (U.S.A.)	1 min 03.98 sec
6. E. Daniel (U.S.A.)	1 min 04.08 sec
7. G. Bukmann (West Germany)	1 min 04.15 sec
8. N. Asano (Japan)	1 min 04.25 sec

200 METRES FREE-STYLE

1. S. Gould (Australia) (World and Olympic record)	2 min 03.56 sec
2. S. Babashoff (U.S.A.)	2 min 04.33 sec
3. K. Rothhammer (U.S.A.)	2 min 04.92 sec
4. A. Marshall (U.S.A.)	2 min 05.45 sec
5. A. Eife (East Germany)	2 min 06.27 sec
6. H. Bunschoten (Netherlands)	2 min 08.40 sec
7. A. Rijnders (Netherlands)	2 min 09.41 sec
8. K. Tuelling (East Germany)	2 min 11.70 sec

800 METRES FREE-STYLE

1. K. Rothammer (U.S.A.) (World and Olympic record)	8 min 53.68 sec
2. S. Gould (Australia)	8 min 56.39 sec
3. N. Calligaris (Italy)	8 min 57.46 sec
4. A. Simmons (U.S.A.)	8 min 57.62 sec
5. G. Wegner (East Germany)	8 min 58.89 sec
6. J. Harsbarger (U.S.A.)	9 min 01.21 sec
7. H. Bunschoten (Netherlands)	9 min 16.69 sec
8. N. Moras (Australia)	9 min 19.06 sec

200 METRES BREASTSTROKE

1. B. Whitfield (Australia) (Olympic record)	2 min 41.71 sec
2. D. Schenfield (U.S.A.)	2 min 42.05 sec
3. G. Stepanova (U.S.S.R.)	2 min 42.36 sec
4. C. Clavenger (U.S.A.)	2 min 42.88 sec
5. P. Nows (West Germany)	2 min 43.38 sec
6. A. Kisne-Kaczander (Hungary)	2 min 43.41 sec
7. L. Porubaiko (U.S.S.R.)	2 min 44.48 sec
8. E. Kiss (Hungary)	2 min 45.12 sec

200 METRES BUTTERFLY

1. K. Moe (U.S.A.) (World and Olympic Record)	2 min 15.57 sec
2. L. Colella (U.S.A.)	2 min 16.34 sec
3. E. Daniel (U.S.A.)	2 min 16.74 sec
4. R. Kother (East Germany)	2 min 17.11 sec
5. N. Asano (Japan)	2 min 19.50 sec
6. H. Lindner (East Germany)	2 min 20.47 sec
7. G. Neall (Australia)	2 min 21.88 sec
8. Mayumi Aoki (Japan)	2 min 22.84 sec

100 METRES BACKSTROKE

1. M. Belote (U.S.A.) (Olympic record)	1 min 5.78 sec
2. A. Gyarmati (Hungary)	1 min 6.26 sec
3. S. Atwood (U.S.A.)	1 min 6.34 sec
4. K. Moe (U.S.A.)	1 min 6.69 sec
5. W. Cook (Canada)	1 min 6.70 sec
6. E. Brigitha (Netherlands)	1 min 6.82 sec
7. C. Herbst (East Germany)	1 min 7.27 sec
8. S. Pielen (West Germany)	1 min 7.36 sec

200 METRES INDIVIDUAL MEDLEY

1. S. Gould (Australia) (World and Olympic record)	2 min 23.07 sec
2. K. Ender (East Germany)	2 min 23.59 sec
3. L. Vidali (U.S.A.)	2 min 24.06 sec
4. J. Bartz (U.S.A.)	2 min 24.55 sec
5. L. Cliff (Canada)	2 min 24.83 sec
6. E. Stolze (East Germany)	2 min 25.90 sec
7. Y. Nishigawa (Japan)	2 min 26.35 sec
8. C. Woods (U.S.A.)	2 min 27.42 sec

4×100 METRES FREE-STYLE RELAY

1. U.S.A. (World and Olympic record)	3 min 55.19 sec
2. East Germany	3 min 55.55 sec
3. West Germany	3 min 57.93 sec
4. Hungary	4 min 00.39 sec
5. Netherlands	4 min 01.49 sec
6. Sweden	4 min 02.69 sec
7. Canada	4 min 03.83 sec
8. Australia	4 min 04.82 sec

SPRINGBOARD DIVING

1. M. King (U.S.A.)	450.03 pts
2. U. Knape (Sweden)	434.19 pts
3. M. Janicke (East Germany)	430.92 pts
4. J. Ely (U.S.A.)	420.99 pts
5. B. Boys (Canada)	418.89 pts
6. A. Henriksson (Sweden)	417.48 pts
7. C. Potter (U.S.A.)	413.58 pts
8. E. Wierniuk (Poland)	408.36 pts
9. H. Becker (East Germany)	405.78 pts
10. M. Duckova (Czechoslovakia)	400.83 pts
11. C. Koehler (East Germany)	394.20 pts
12. A. Drake (G.B.)	378.81 pts

200 METRES BACKSTROKE

1. M. Belote (U.S.A.) (World and Olympic record)	2 min 19.19 sec
2. S. Atwood (U.S.A.)	2 min 20.38 sec
3. D. M. Gurr (Canada)	2 min 23.22 sec
4. A. Kober (West Germany)	2 min 23.35 sec
5. C. Herbst (East Germany)	2 min 23.44 sec
6. E. Brigitha (Netherlands)	2 min 23.70 sec
7. D. Palmer (Australia)	2 min 24.65 sec
8. L. Cliff (Canada)	2 min 25.80 sec

400 METRES INDIVIDUAL MEDLEY

1. G. Neal (Australia) (World and Olympic record)	5 min 02.97 sec
2. L. Cliff (Canada)	5 min 03.57 sec
3. N. Calligaris (Italy)	5 min 03.99 sec
4. J. Bartz (U.S.A.)	5 min 05.56 sec
5. E. Stoize (East Germany)	5 min 06.80 sec
6. M. Montgomery (U.S.A.)	5 min 09.98 sec
7. L. Vidali (U.S.A.)	5 min 13.06 sec
8. N. Petrova (U.S.S.R.)	5 min 15.68 sec

400 METRES MEDLEY RELAY

1. U.S.A. (World and Olympic record)	4 min 20.75 sec
2. East Germany	4 min 24.91 sec
3. West Germany	4 min 26.46 sec
4. U.S.S.R.	4 min 27.81 sec
5. Netherlands	4 min 29.99 sec
6. Japan	4 min 30.18 sec
7. Canada	4 min 31.56 sec
8. Sweden	4 min 32.61 sec

HIGHBOARD DIVING

1. U. Knape (Sweden)	390.00 pts
2. M. Duchkova (Czechoslovakia)	370.92 pts
3. M. Janicke (East Germany)	360.54 pts
4. J. Ely (U.S.A.)	352.68 pts
5. M. King (U.S.A.)	346.38 pts
6. S. Fiedler (East Germany)	341.67 pts
7. N. Robertson (Canada)	334.02 pts
8. I. Pertmayr (Austria)	321.03 pts
12. B. Williams (G.B.)	301.26 pts

WATER POLO

1. U.S.S.R.
2. Hungary
3. U.S.A.
4. West Germany
5. Yugoslavia
6. Italy
7. Netherlands
8. Rumania
9. Cuba
10. Spain
11. Bulgaria
12. Australia

BOXING

LIGHT-FLYWEIGHT

1. G. Gedo (Hungary)
2. U. G. Kim (North Korea)
3. R. Evans (G.B.)
3. E. Rodriguez (Spain)

FLYWEIGHT

1. G. Kostadinov (Bulgaria)
2. E. Rwabwogo (Uganda)
3. L. Blazynski (Poland)
3. D. Rodriguez (Cuba)

BANTAMWEIGHT
1. O. Martinez (Cuba)
2. A. Zamora (Mexico)
3. G. Turpin (G.B.)
3. R. Carreras (U.S.A.)

FEATHERWEIGHT
1. B. Kousnetsov (U.S.S.R.)
2. P. Waruinge (Kenya)
3. C. Rojas (Colombia)
3. A. Botos (Hungary)

LIGHTWEIGHT
1. J. Szczepanski (Poland)
2. L. Orban (Hungary)
3. S. Mbugua (Kenya)
3. A. Perez (Colombia)

LIGHT-WELTERWEIGHT
1. R. Seales (U.S.A.)
2. A. Anghelov (Bulgaria)
3. Z. Vujin (Yugoslavia)
3. I. Daborg (Niger)

WELTERWEIGHT
1. E. Correa (Cuba)
2. J. Kajdi (Hungary)
3. D. Murunga (Kenya)
3. J. Valdez (U.S.A.)

LIGHT-MIDDLEWEIGHT
1. D. Kottysch (West Germany)
2. W. Rudkowski (Poland)
3. A. Minter (G.B.)
3. P. Tiepold (East Germany

MIDDLEWEIGHT
1. V. Lemenchev (U.S.S.R.)
2. R. Virtanen (Finland)
3. P. Amartey (Ghana)
3. M. Johnson (U.S.A.)

LIGHT-HEAVYWEIGHT
1. M. Parlov (Yugoslavia)
2. G. Carrillo (Cuba)
3. I. Ikhouria (Nigeria)
3. J. Gorat (Poland)

HEAVYWEIGHT
1. T. Stevenson (Cuba)
2. I. Alexe (Rumania)
3. P. Hussing (West Germany)
3. H. Thomsen (Sweden)

Note: Two Bronze medals were awarded in each of the eleven categories of the Boxing tournament.

WRESTLING

Graeco-Roman

LIGHT-FLYWEIGHT
1. G. Berceasu (Rumania
2. R. Aliabadi (Iran)
3. S. Anghelov (Bulgaria)

FLYWEIGHT
1. P. Kirov (Bulgaria)
2. K. Hirayama (Japan)
3. G. Bognanni (Italy)

BANTAMWEIGHT
1. R. Kazakov (U.S.S.R.)
2. H. Veil (West Germany)
3. R. Bjoerlin (Finland)

FEATHERWEIGHT
1. G. Markov (Bulgaria)
2. H. Wehling (East Germany)
3. K. Lipien (Poland)

LIGHTWEIGHT
1. S. Khisamutdinov (U.S.S.R.)
2. S. Apostolov (Bulgaria)
3. G. Ranzi (Italy)

WELTERWEIGHT
1. V. Macha (Czechoslovakia)
2. P. Galaktopoulos (Greece)
3. J. Karlsson (Sweden)

MIDDLEWEIGHT
1. C. Hegedus (Hungary)
2. A. Nazarenko (U.S.S.R.)
3. M. Nenadic (Yugoslavia)

LIGHT-HEAVYWEIGHT
1. V. Rezantsev (U.S.S.R.)
2. J. Corak (Yugoslavia)
3. C. Kwiecinski (Poland)

HEAVYWEIGHT
1. N. Martinescu (Rumania)
2. N. Iakovenko (U.S.S.R.)
3. F. Kiss (Hungary)

SUPER-HEAVYWEIGHT
1. A. Roshin (U.S.S.R.)
2. A. Tomov (Bulgaria)
3. V. Dolipschi (Rumania)

Free-style

LIGHT-FLYWEIGHT
1. R. Dmitriev (U.S.S.R.)
2. O. Nikolov (Bulgaria)
3. E. Jauadpour (Iran)

BANTAMWEIGHT
1. H. Yanagida (Japan)
2. R. Sanders (U.S.A.)
3. L. Klinga (Hungary)

LIGHTWEIGHT
1. D. Gable (U.S.A.)
2. K. Wada (Japan)
3. R. Ashuraliev (U.S.S.R.)

MIDDLEWEIGHT
1. L. Tedioshvili (U.S.S.R.)
2. J. Peterson (U.S.A.)
3. V. Jorga (Rumania)

HEAVYWEIGHT
1. I. Yarygin (U.S.S.R.)
2. K. Baianmunkh (Mongolia)
3. J. Csatari (Hungary)

FLYWEIGHT
1. K. Kato (Japan)
2. A. Alakhverdiev (U.S.S.R.)
3. H. K. Gwong (North Korea)

FEATHERWEIGHT
1. Z. Abdulbekov (U.S.S.R.)
2. V. Akdag (Turkey)
3. I. Krastev (Bulgaria)

WELTERWEIGHT
1. W. Wells (U.S.A.)
2. A. Karlsson (Sweden)
3. A. Seger (West Germany)

LIGHT-HEAVYWEIGHT
1. B. Peterson (U.S.A.)
2. G. Strakhov (U.S.S.R.)
3. K. Bajko (Hungary)

SUPER-HEAVYWEIGHT
1. A. Medved (U.S.S.R.)
2. O. Douraliev (Bulgaria)
3. C. Taylor (U.S.A.)

JUDO

LIGHTWEIGHT
1. T. Kawaguchi (Japan)
2. Withheld
3. Y. I. Kim (North Korea)
3. I. Mounier (France)

MIDDLEWEIGHT
1. S. Sekine (Japan)
2. S. L. Oh (North Korea)
3. B. Jacks (G.B.)
3. J. Coche (France)

HEAVYWEIGHT
1. W. Ruska (Netherlands)
2. D. Glahn (West Germany)
3. G. Onashvili (U.S.S.R.)
3. M. Nishimura (Japan)

WELTERWEIGHT
1. T. Nomura (Japan)
2. A. Zajkowski (Poland)
3. D. Hoetger (East Germany
3. A. Novikov (U.S.S.R.)

MIDDLE-HEAVY
1. S. Chochoshvili (U.S.S.R.
2. D. Starbrook (G.B.)
3. P. Barth (West Germany)
3. C. Ishii (Brazil)

OPEN
1. W. Ruska (Netherlands)
2. V. Kusnezov (U.S.S.R.)
3. A. Parisi (G.B.)
3. J. Brondani (France)

Note: B. Buidaa (Mongolia) who came second in the Lightweight division was disqualified after his dope test had proved positive. The Silver medal was withheld.

Two Bronze medals were awarded in each of the six categories of the Judo tournament.

WEIGHT-LIFTING

FLYWEIGHT

1. Z. Smalcerz (Poland)	743¾ lb
2. L. Szuecs (Hungary)	727 lb
3. S. Holczreiter (Hungary)	721¾ lb
4. T. Sasaki (Japan)	710¾ lb
5. G. Aung (Bermuda)	705¼ lb
6. Dong Geun Pak (North Korea)	699¾ lb
7. Chaiy Sukchinda (Thailand)	688½ lb
8. I. Hortopan (Rumania)	683 lb

BANTAMWEIGHT

1. I. Foeldi (Hungary)	831¾ lb
2. M. Nassiri (Iran)	815¼ lb
3. G. Chetin (U.S.S.R.)	809¾ lb
9. P. McKenzie (G.B.)	754¾ lb

FEATHERWEIGHT

1. N. Nourikian (Bulgaria) (equals World and Olympic record)	887 lb
2. D. Shanidze (U.S.S.R.)	881½ lb
3. J. Benedek (Hungary)	859½ lb

MIDDLEWEIGHT

1. Y. Bikov (Bulgaria) (World and Olympic record)	1,068¾ lb
2. M. Trabulsi (Lebanon)	1,041¼ lb
3. A. Silvano (Italy)	1,035¾ lb

MIDDLE-HEAVYWEIGHT

1. A. Nikolov (Bulgaria) (Olympic record)	1,157 lb
2. A. Chopov (Bulgaria)	1,140½ lb
3. H. Bettenbourg (Sweden)	1,129½ lb
15. P. Arthur (G.B.)	1,002¾ lb

LIGHTWEIGHT

1. M. Kirzinov (U.S.S.R.) (World and Olympic record)	1,013¾ lb
2. M. Koutchev (Bulgaria)	991¾ lb
3. Z. Kacmarek (Poland)	975¼ lb
15. G. Newton (G.B.)	887 lb
18. I. Owen (G.B.)	832¾ lb

LIGHT-HEAVYWEIGHT

1. L. Jensen (Norway) (Olympic record)	1,118¾ lb
2. N. Ozimek (Poland)	1,096¾ lb
3. G. Horvath (Hungary)	1,091 lb
11. M. Pearman (G.B.)	959 lb
13. T. Ford (G.B.)	959 lb

HEAVYWEIGHT

1. Y. Talts (U.S.S.R.)	1,278¼ lb
2. A. Kraitchev (Bulgaria)	1.239½ lb
3. S. Gruetzner (East Germany)	1,223 lb
13. D. Hancock (G.B.)	1,124½ lb
18. K. Price (G.B.)	1,058 lb

SUPER-HEAVYWEIGHT

1. V. Alexeyev (U.S.S.R.) (Olympic record)	1,409¼ lb
2. R. Mang (West Germany)	1,344½ lb
3. G. Bonk (East Germany)	1,261¾ lb
10. T. Perdue (G.B.)	1,129½ lb

GYMNASTICS

Men

FLOOR EXERCISES

1. N. Andrianov (U.S.S.R.)	19.175 pts
2. A. Nakayama (Japan)	19.125 pts
3. S. Kasamatsu (Japan)	19.025 pts
4. E. Kenmotsu (Japan)	18.925 pts
5. K. Koeste (East Germany)	18.825 pts
6. S. Kato (Japan)	18.750 pts

LONG HORSE

1. K. Koeste (East Germany)	18.850 pts
2. V. Klimenko (U.S.S.R.)	18.825 pts
3. N. Andrianov (U.S.S.R.)	18.800 pts
4. E. Kenmotsu (Japan)	18.550 pts
S. Kato (Japan)	18.550 pts
6. P. Rohner (Switzerland)	18.525 pts

PARALLEL BARS

1. S. Kato (Japan)	19.475 pts
2. S. Kasamatsu (Japan)	19.375 pts
3. E. Kenmotsu (Japan)	19.250 pts
4. V. Klimenko (U.S.S.R.)	19.125 pts
5. A. Nakayama (Japan)	18.875 pts
6. N. Andrianov (U.S.S.R.)	17.975 pts

POMMELLED HORSE

1. V. Klimenko (U.S.S.R.)	19.125 pts
2. S. Kato (Japan)	19.000 pts
3. E. Kenmotsu (Japan)	18.950 pts
4. S. Kasamatsu (Japan)	18.925 pts
5. M. Voronin (U.S.S.R.)	18.875 pts
6. W. Kubica (Poland)	18.750 pts

HORIZONTAL BARS

1. M. Tsukuhara (Japan)	19.725 pts
2. S. Kato (Japan)	19.525 pts
3. S. Kasamatsu (Japan)	19.450 pts
4. E. Kenmotsu (Japan)	19.350 pts
5. A. Nakayama (Japan)	19.225 pts
6. N. Andrianov (U.S.S.R.)	19.100 pts

RINGS

1. A. Nakayama (Japan)	19.350 pts
2. M. Voronin (U.S.S.R.)	19.275 pts
3. M. Tsukahara (Japan)	19.225 pts
4. S. Kato (Japan)	19.150 pts
5. E. Kenmotsu (Japan)	18.950 pts
K. Koeste (East Germany)	18.950 pts

COMBINED INDIVIDUAL EXERCISES

1. S. Kato (Japan)	114.650 pts
2. E. Kenmotsu (Japan)	114.575 pts
3. N. Nakayama (Japan)	114.325 pts
4. N. Andrianov (U.S.S.R.)	114.200 pts
5. S. Kasamatsu (Japan)	113.700 pts
6. K. Koeste (East Germany)	113.075 pts
V. Klimenko (U.S.S.R.)	113.075 pts
8. M. Tsukahara (Japan)	112.775 pts

TEAM CHAMPIONSHIP

1. Japan	571.25 pts
2. U.S.S.R.	564.05 pts
3. East Germany	559.70 pts
4. Poland	551.10 pts
5. West Germany	546.40 pts
6. North Korea	545.05 pts
7. Rumania	538.90 pts
8. Hungary	538.60 pts

GYMNASTICS

Women

ASYMMETRICAL BARS

1. K. Janz (East Germany)	19.675 pts
2. O. Korbut (U.S.S.R.)	19.450 pts
E. Zuchold (East Germany)	19.450 pts
4. L. Turischeva (U.S.S.R.)	19.425 pts
5. I. Bekesi (Hungary)	19.275 pts
6. A. Hellman (East Germany)	19.200 pts

FLOOR EXERCISES

1. O. Korbut (U.S.S.R.)	19.575 pts
2. L. Turischeva (U.S.S.R.)	19.550 pts
3. T. Lazakovitch (U.S.S.R.)	19.450 pts
4. K. Janz (East Germany)	19.400 pts
5. L. Burda U.S.S.R.)	19.100 pts
A. Hellmann (East Germany)	19.100 pts

COMBINED INDIVIDUAL EXERCISES

1. L. Turischeva (U.S.S.R.)	77.025 pts
2. K. Janz (East Germany)	76.875 pts
3. T. Lazakovitch (U.S.S.R.)	76.850 pts
4. E. Zuchold (East Germany)	76.450 pts
5. L. Burda (U.S.S.R.)	75.775 pts
6. A. Hellmann (East Germany)	75.550 pts
7. O. Korbut (U.S.S.R.)	75.100 pts
8. E. Saadi (U.S.S.R.)	75.075 pts

LONG HORSE

1. K. Janz (East Germany)	19.525 pts
2. E. Zuchold (East Germany)	19.275 pts
3. L. Turischeva (U.S.S.R.)	19.250 pts
4. L. Burda (U.S.S.R.)	19.225 pts
5. O. Korbut (U.S.S.R.)	19.175 pts
6. T. Lazakovitch (U.S.S.R.)	19.050 pts

BEAM

1. O. Korbut (U.S.S.R.)	19.400 pts
2. T. Lazakovitch (U.S.S.R.)	19.375 pts
3. K. Janz (East Germany)	18.975 pts
4. M. Csaszar (Hungary)	18.925 pts
5. L. Turischeva (U.S.S.R.)	18.800 pts
6. E. Zuchold (East Germany)	18.700 pts

TEAM CHAMPIONSHIP

1. U.S.S.R.	380.50 pts
2. East Germany	376.55 pts
3. Hungary	368.25 pts
4. U.S.A.	365.90 pts
5. Czechoslovakia	365.00 pts
6. Rumania	360.70 pts
7. Japan	359.75 pts
8. West Germany	355.95 pts
18. G.B.	333.95 pts

CYCLING

1000 METRES TIME TRIAL

1. N. Fredbord (Denmark)	1 min 06.44 sec
2. D. Clark (Australia)	1 min 06.87 sec
3. J. Schuetz (East Germany)	1 min 07.02 sec
4. K. Koethr (West Germany)	1 min 07.21 sec
5. J. Kierzkowski (Poland)	1 min 07.22 sec
6. D. Tontchev (Bulgaria)	1 min 07.55 sec
7. C. Brunner (Switzerland)	1 min 07.71 sec
8. E. Rapp (U.S.S.R.)	1 min 07.73 sec

TANDEM SPRINT

1. U.S.S.R.
2. East Germany
3. Poland
4. France

1000 METRES SPRINT

1. N. Fredborg (Denmark)	1 min 6.44 sec
2. D. Clark (Australia)	1 min 6.87 sec
3. J. Schuetze (East Germany)	1 min 7.02 sec
4. K. Koether (West Germany)	1 min 7.21 sec
17. M. Bennett (G.B.)	1 min 9.45 sec

4000 METRES INDIVIDUAL PURSUIT

1. K. Knudsen (Norway)	4 min 45.74 sec
2. X. Kurmann (Switzerland)	4 min 51.96 sec
3. H. Lutz (West Germany)	4 min 50.80 sec
4. J. Bylsma (Australia)	4 min 54.93 sec

TEAM PURSUIT

1. West Germany	4 min 22.14 sec
2. East Germany	4 min 25.25 sec
3. G.B.	4 min 23.78 sec
4. Poland	4 min 25.06 sec

100 KILOMETRES TEAM TIME TRIAL

1. U.S.S.R.	2 hr 11 min 17.8 sec
2. Poland	2 hr 11 min 47.5 sec
3. Netherlands	2 hr 12 min 27.1 sec
4. Belgium	2 hr 12 min 36.7 sec
5. Norway	2 hr 13 min 20.7 sec
6. Sweden	2 hr 13 min 36.9 sec
7. Hungary	2 hr 14 min 18.8 sec
8. Switzerland	2 hr 14 min 33.6 sec
14. G.B.	2 hr 16 min 18.0 sec

Note: The Dutch team, who came third in the 100 Kilometres Time Trial, were disqualified for taking drugs. The Bronze medal in this event was withheld.

INDIVIDUAL ROAD RACE

1. H. Kuyper (Netherlands)	4 hr 14 min 37.0 sec
2. K. Sefton (Australia)	4 hr 15 min 04.0 sec
3. J. Huelmaomo (Spain)	4 hr 15 min 04.0 sec
4. B. Biddle (New Zealand)	4 hr 15 min 04.0 sec
5. P. Bayton (G.B.)	4 hr 15 min 34.0 sec
6. P. Edwards (G.B.)	4 hr 16 min 10.0 sec
7. W. Trott (West Germany)	4 hr 16 min 10.0 sec
F. Moser (Italy)	4 hr 16 min 10.0 sec
9. M. Samaca (Colombia)	4 hr 16 min 54.0 sec
J. Sarabia (Mexico)	4 hr 16 min 54.0 sec

CANOEING—SLALOM

Men

KAYAK SINGLES

1. S. Horn (East Germany)	4 min 28.56 sec
2. N. Sattler (Austria)	4 min 30.76 sec
3. H. Gimpel (East Germany)	4 min 37.95 sec
4. U. Peters (West Germany)	4 min 42.82 sec
5. A. Baum (West Germany)	4 min 48.01 sec
6. M. Havlicke (Czechoslovakia)	4 min 49.56 sec
7. E. Evans (U.S.A.)	4 min 56.34 sec
8. J. Bremer (East Germany)	5 min 03.15 sec
22. D. Mitchell (G.B.)	5 min 43.02 sec
30. J. Macleod (G.B.)	6 min 38.99 sec
32. R. Calverly (G.B.)	6 min 50.80 sec

CANADIAN SINGLES

1. R. Eiben (East Germany)	5 min 15.84 sec
2. R. Kauder (West Germany)	5 min 27.89 sec
3. J. McEwan (U.S.A.)	5 min 33.95 sec
4. J. Foerster (East Germany)	5 min 54.42 sec
5. W. Peters (West Germany)	5 min 56.25 sec
6. J. Koehler (East Germany)	6 min 12.88 sec
7. K. Tresnak (Czechoslovakia)	6 min 25.07 sec
8. P. Sodomka (Czechoslovakia)	6 min 31.11 sec

CANADIAN PAIRS

1. W. Hofmann and R.-D. Amend (East Germany)	310.68 pts
2. H. O. Schumacher and W. Baues (West Germany)	311.90 pts
3. J.-L. Olry and J.-C. Olry (France)	315.10 pts
4. J. Kretschmer and K. Trummer (East Germany)	329.57 pts
5. J. Fraczek and R. Seruga (Poland)	366.21 pts
6. J. Andrijasic and P. Guzelf (Yugoslavia)	368.01 pts
7. M. Reimann and O. Fricke (West Germany)	371.86 pts
8. H. Muellneritsch and H. Steindl (Austria)	375.14 pts
15. D. Allen and L. Williams (G.B.)	447.08 pts

Women

KAYAK SINGLES

1. A. Bahmann (East Germany)	364.50 pts
2. G. Grothaus (West Germany)	398.15 pts
3. M. Wunderlich (West Germany)	400.50 pts
4. M. Cwiertniewicz (Poland)	432.30 pts
5. K. Goodawska (Poland)	441.05 pts
6. V. Brown (G.B.)	443.71 pts
7. U. Deppe (West Germany)	456.44 pts
8. B. Kepplova (Czechoslovakia)	450.16 pts
13. H. Goodman (G.B.)	527.50 pts
21. P. Squires-Goodwin (G.B.)	673.60 pts

CANOEING—STRAIGHT RACES

Men

KAYAK SINGLES

1. A. Shaparenko (U.S.S.R.)	3 min 48.06 sec
2. R. Peterson (Sweden)	3 min 48.35 sec
3. G. Csapo (Hungary)	3 min 49.38 sec
4. J.-P. Burny (Belgium)	3 min 50.29 sec
5. L. Soucek (Czechoslovakia)	3 min 51.05 sec
6. J. Mattern (East Germany)	3 min 51.94 sec

KAYAK PAIRS

1. N. Gorbachev and V. Kratassyuk (U.S.S.R.)	3 min 31.23 sec
2. J. Deme and J. Ratkai (Hungary)	3 min 32.00 sec
3. W. Szuszkiewicz and R. Piszcz (Poland)	3 min 33.83 sec
4. R. Kurth and A. Slatnow (East Germany)	3 min 34.16 sec
5. C. Cosnita and V. Simiocenco (Rumania)	3 min 35.66 sec
6. J.-P. Cordebois and D. Niquet (France)	3 min 36.51 sec

KAYAK FOURS

1. U.S.S.R.	3 min 14.02 sec
2. Rumania	3 min 15.07 sec
3. Norway	3 min 15.27 sec
4. Italy	3 min 15.60 sec
5. West Germany	3 min 16.63 sec
6. Hungary	3 min 16.88 sec

CANADIAN SINGLES

1. I. Patzaichin (Rumania)	4 min 08.94 sec
2. T. Wichmann (Hungary)	4 min 12.42 sec
3. D. Lewe (West Germany)	4 min 13.63 sec
4. D. Weise (East Germany)	4 min 14.38 sec
5. V. Yurchenko (U.S.S.R.)	4 min 14.43 sec
6. B. Lubenov (Bulgaria)	4 min 14.65 sec

CANADIAN PAIRS

1. V. Chessyunas and Y. Lobanov (U.S.S.R.)	3 min 52.60 sec
2. I. Patzaichin and S. Covaliov (Rumania)	3 min 52.63 sec
3. F. Damianov and I. Bourtchine (Bulgaria)	3 min 58,10 sec
4. H.-P. Hoffmann and H. Glaser (West Germany)	3 min 59.24 sec
5. M. Darvas and P. Povazsay (Hungary)	4 min 00.42 sec
6. R. Muhlen and A. Weigand (U.S.A.)	4 min 01.28 sec

Women

KAYAK SINGLES

1. Y. Ryabchinskaya (U.S.S.R.)	2 min 03.17 sec
2. M. Jaapies (Netherlands)	2 min 04.03 sec
3. A. Pfeffer (Hungary)	2 min 05.50 sec
4. I. Pepinhege (West Germany)	2 min 06.55 sec
5. B. Mueller (East Germany)	2 min 06.85 sec
6. M. Nichiforov (Rumania)	2 min 07.13 sec

KAYAK PAIRS

1. L. Pinayeva and E. Kuryshko (U.S.S.R.)	1 min 53.50 sec
2. I. Kaschube and P. Grabowsky (East Germany)	1 min 54.30 sec
3. M. Nichiforov and V. Dumitru (Rumania)	1 min 55.01 sec
4. Hungary	1 min 55.12 sec
5. West Germany	1 min 55.64 sec
6. Poland	1 min 57.45 sec

ROWING

EIGHTS

1. New Zealand	6 min 08.94 sec
2. U.S.A.	6 min 11.61 sec
3. East Germany	6 min 11.67 sec

COXLESS FOURS

1. East Germany	6 min 24.27 sec
2. New Zealand	6 min 25.64 sec
3. West Germany	6 min 28.41 sec

COXLESS PAIRS

1. S. Brietzke and W. Mager (East Germany)	6 min 53.16 sec
2. A. Bachmann and H. Fischer (Switzerland)	6 min 57.06 sec
3. R. Luynenburg and R. Stokvis (Netherlands)	6 min 58.70 sec

COXED FOURS

1. West Germany	6 min 31.85 sec
2. East Germany	6 min 33.30 sec
3. Czechoslovakia	6 min 35.64 sec

COXED PAIRS

1. East Germany	7 min 17.25 sec
2. Czechoslovakia	7 min 19.57 sec
3. Rumania	7 min 21.36 sec

DOUBLE SCULLS

1. A. Timoshinin and G. Korshiko (U.S.S.R.)	7 min 01.77 sec
2. F. Hensen and S. Thogersen (Norway)	7 min 02.58 sec
3. J. Bochmer and H. U. Schmied (East Germany)	7 min 05.55 sec
5. T. Crooks and P. Delafield (G.B.)	7 min 16.29 sec

SINGLE SCULLS

1. Y. Malishev (U.S.S.R.)	7 min 10.12 sec
2. A. Demiddi (Argentina)	7 min 11.53 sec
3. W. Gueldenpfennig (East Germany)	7 min 14.45 sec

YACHTING

FINN

1. France	58.0 pts
2. Greece	71.0 pts
3. U.S.S.R.	74.7 pts
4. Australia	76.7 pts
5. Sweden	81.0 pts
6. Finland	85.7 pts
7. East Germany	91.0 pts
8. Hungary	94.0 pts
9. Brazil	105.7 pts
10. New Zealand	109.7 pts
18. G.B.	133.7 pts

TEMPEST

1. U.S.S.R.	28.1 pts
2. G.B.	34.4 pts
3. U.S.A.	47.7 pts
4. Sweden	57.4 pts
5. Netherlands	58.7 pts
6. Norway	70.0 pts
7. Brazil	73.7 pts
8. Ireland	74.7 pts
9. France	78.0 pts
10. Austria	84.4 pts

SOLING

1. U.S.A.	8.7 pts
2. Sweden	31.7 pts
3. Canada	47.1 pts
4. France	53.0 pts
5. G.B.	54.7 pts
6. Brazil	64.7 pts
7. U.S.S.R.	65.0 pts
8. Poland	75.0 pts
9. Spain	76.0 pts
10. Norway	76.7 pts

FLYING DUTCHMAN

1. G.B.	22.7 pts
2. France	40.7 pts
3. West Germany	51.1 pts
4. Brazil	62.4 pts
5. Yugoslavia	63.7 pts
6. U.S.S.R.	67.7 pts
7. Denmark	74.4 pts
8. Australia	75.7 pts
9. New Zealand	79.0 pts
10. Netherlands	96.0 pts

STAR

1. Australia	28.1 pts
2. Sweden	44.0 pts
3. West Germany	44.4 pts
4. Brazil	52.7 pts
5. Italy	58.4 pts
6. Portugal	68.4 pts
7. G.B.	68.7 pts
8. Hungary	74.0 pts
9. U.S.S.R.	76.0 ots
10. U.S.A.	89.0 pts

DRAGON

1. Australia	13.7 pts
2. East Germany	41.7 pts
3. U.S.A.	47.7 pts
4. West Germany	47.7 pts
5. New Zealand	51.0 pts
6. Sweden	67.4 pts
7. Denmark	68.0 pts
8. Finland	68.7 pts
9. Canada	69.0 pts
10. Austria	71.7 pts
12. G.B.	78.7 pts

EQUESTRIAN

THREE-DAY EVENT (INDIVIDUAL)

1. R. Meade (G.B.) (Laurieston)	57.73 pts
2. A. Argenton (Italy) (Woodland)	43.33 pts
3. J. Jonsson (Sweden) (Sarajevo)	39.67 pts
4. Miss M. Gordon-Watson (G.B.) (Cornishman V)	30.27 pts
5. K. Freeman (U.S.A.) (Good Mixture)	29.87 pts
6. W. Roycroft (Australia) (Warrathoola)	29.60 pts
7. R. Sands (Australia) (Deeche)	24.87 pts
8. B. Davidson (U.S.A.) (Plain Sailing)	24.47 pts
9. H. Klugmann (West Germany) (Christopher Rob)	8.00 pts
10. Mrs B. Parker (G.B.) (Cornish Gold)	7.53 pts
35. M. Phillips (G.B.) (Great Ovation)	—134.33 pts

THREE-DAY EVENT (TEAM)

1. G.B.	95.53 pts
2. U.S.A.	10.31 pts
3. West Germany	—18.00 pts
4. Australia	—27.86 pts
5. East Germany	—127.93 pts
6. Switzerland	—156.43 pts
7. U.S.S.R.	—190.06 pts
8. Italy	—203.58 pts
9. Ireland	—219.41 pts
10. Poland	—281.60 pts
11. France	—338.56 pts
12. Austria	—485.60 pts

INDIVIDUAL JUMPING—GRAND PRIX DES NATIONS

1. G. Mancinelli (Italy) (Ambassador)	8.00 faults
2. A. Moore (G.B.) (Psalm)	8.00 faults
3. N. Shapiro (U.S.A.) (Sloppy)	8.00 faults
4. J. Day (Canada) (Steelmaster)	8.75 faults
S. Hugo (Austria) (Lavendel)	8.75 faults
H. Steenken (West Germany) (Simons)	8.75 faults
7. J.-M. Rozier (Italy) (Sans Souci)	12.00 faults
8. A. Segovia (Spain) (Tic Tac)	16.00 faults
F. Ligges (West Germany) (Robin)	16.00 faults
14. D. Broome (G.B.) (Manhattan)	21.25 faults
15. M. Saywell (G.B.) (Hideaway)	24.25 faults

TEAM JUMPING—GRAND PRIX DES NATIONS

1. West Germany	32 faults
2. U.S.A.	32.25 faults
3. Italy	48 faults
4. G.B. (H. Smith (Summertime); M. Saywell (Hideaway); A. Moore (Psalm); D. Broome (Manhattan VI))	51 faults
5. Switzerland	61.25 faults
6. Canada	64 faults
7. Spain	66 faults
8. Argentina	121 faults

INDIVIDUAL—GRAND PRIX DE DRESSAGE

1. Linsenholf (West Germany) (Piaff)	1229 pts
2. E. Petushkova (U.S.S.R.) (Pepel)	1185 pts
3. J. Neckerman (West Germany) (Venetia)	1177 pts
4. I. Kizimov (U.S.S.R.) (Ikhor)	1159 pts
5. I. Kalita (U.S.S.R.) (Tarif)	1130 pts
6. U. Hakansson (Sweden) (Ajax)	1126 pts
7. K. Schlueter (West Germany) (Liostro)	1113 pts
8. M. Von Rosen (Sweden) (Lucky Boy)	1088 pts
12. L. Johnstone (G.B.) (El Farruco)	1036 pts

TEAM—GRAND PRIX DE DRESSAGE

1. U.S.S.R.	5095 pts
2. West Germany	5083 pts
3. Sweden	4849 pts
4. Denmark	4606 pts
5. East Germany	4552 pts
6. Canada	4418 pts
7. Switzerland	4383 pts
8. Netherlands	4309 pts
9. U.S.A.	4283 pts
10. G.B. (L. Johnstone, J. Loriston-Clarke, D. Lawrence)	4268 pts

ARCHERY

MEN

288 arrows (72 each at 90 metres, 70 metres, 50 metres and 30 metres)

1. J. Williams (U.S.A.)	2538 pts
2. G. Jervill (Sweden)	2481 pts
3. K. Laasonon (Finland)	2467 pts
4. R. Cogniaux (Belgium)	2445 pts
5. E. Eliason (U.S.A.)	2438 pts
6. D. Jackson (Canada)	2437 pts
17. R. Matthews (G.B.)	2385 pts
26. J. Snelling (G.B.)	2356 pts
45. R. Bishop (G.B.)	2244 pts

WOMEN

288 arrows (72 each at 70 metres, 60 metres, 50 metres and 30 metres)

1. D. Wilber (U.S.A.)	2424 pts
2. I. Szydlowska (Poland)	2407 pts
3. E. Gaptchenko (U.S.S.R.)	2403 pts
4. K. Lossabridz (U.S.S.R.)	2402 pts
5. L. Myers (U.S.A.)	2385 pts
6. M. Maczynska (Poland)	2371 pts
16. L. Evans (G.B.)	2313 pts
21. C. Sykes (G.B.)	2275 pts
25. P. Edwards (G.B.)	2249 pts

FENCING

Men

TEAM EPEE
1. Hungary
2. Switzerland
3. U.S.S.R.
4. France

TEAM FOIL
1. Poland
2. U.S.S.R.
3. France
4. Hungary
5. West Germany
6. Japan

TEAM SABRE
1. Italy
2. U.S.S.R.
3. Hungary
4. Rumania
5. Poland
6. Cuba

INDIVIDUAL EPEE

1. C. Fenyvesi (Hungary)	4 wins
2. J. La Degaillerie (France)	3 wins
3. Kulscar (Hungary)	3 wins
4. A. Pongratz (Rumania)	3 wins
5. R. Edling (Sweden)	1 win
6. J. Brodin (France)	0 win

INDIVIDUAL FOIL

1. W. Wyoda (Poland)	5 wins
2. J. Kamuti (Hungary)	4 wins
3. C. Noel (France)	2 wins
4. M. Tiu (Rumania)	2 wins
5. V. Denissov (U.S.S.R.)	2 wins
6. M. Dabrowski (Poland)	0 win

INDIVIDUAL SABRE

1. V. Sidiak (U.S.S.R.)	4 wins
2. P. Maroth (Hungary)	3 wins
3. V. Nazylmov (U.S.S.R.)	3 wins
4. M. Maffei (Italy)	3 wins
5. R. Bonissent (France)	1 win
6. T. Kouacs (Hungary)	1 win

Women

TEAM FOIL
1. U.S.S.R.
2. Hungary
3. Rumania
4. Italy
5. West Germany
6. France

INDIVIDUAL FOIL

1. A. Ragno Lonzi (Italy)	4 wins
2. I. Bobis (Hungary)	3 wins
3. G. Gorokhova (U.S.S.R.)	3 wins
4. M.-C. Demaille (France)	3 wins
5. E. Belova (U.S.S.R.)	2 wins
6. K. Palm (Sweden)	0 win

SHOOTING

FREE PISTOL

1. R. Skanaker (Sweden) 567 pts
   (Olympic record)
2. D. Iuga (Rumania) 562 pts
3. R. Dollinger (Austria) 560 pts
4. R. Stachurski (Poland) 559 pts
5. H. Vollmar (East Germany) 558 pts
6. H. Hromada (Czechoslovakia) 556 pts
7. K. Marosvari (Hungary) 555 pts
8. G. Kosykh (U.S.S.R.) 555 pts

14. R. Wyatt (G.B.) 552 pts
31. H. Cullum (G.B.) 542 pts

FREE RIFLE

1. L. Wigger (U.S.A.) 1155 pts
2. B. Melnik (U.S.S.R.) 1155 pts
3. L. Pap (Hungary) 1149 pts
4. U. Wunderlich (East Germany) 1149 pts
5. K. Bulan (Czechoslovakia) 1146 pts
6. J. Minkkinen (Finland) 1146 pts
7. L. Bassham (U.S.A.) 1144 pts
8. V. Kormev (U.S.S.R.) 1143 pts

12. M. Cooper (G.B.) 1139 pts

SMALL-BORE RIFLE: THREE POSITIONS

1. J. Writer (U.S.A.) 1166 pts
   (World record)
2. K. Bassham (U.S.A.) 1157 pts
3. W. Lippoldt (East Germany) 1153 pts
4. P. Kovarik (Czechoslovakia) 1153 pts
5. V. Agishev (U.S.S.R.) 1152 pts
6. A. Sieledcow (Poland) 1151 pts
7. G. Kustermann (West Germany) 1149 pts
8. N. Rotaru (Rumania) 1148 pts

18. M. Cooper (G.B.) 1141 pts
31. R. Churchill (G.B.) 1132 pts

SKEET

1. K. Wirnhier (West Germany) 195 pts
2. E. Petrov (U.S.S.R.) 195 pts
3. M. Buchheim (East Germany) 195 pts
   (after shoot-off)
4. J. Neville (G.B.) 194 pts
5. R. Castrillo (Cuba) 194 pts
6. K. Reschke (East Germany) 193 pts
7. E. Penot (France) 193 pts
8. P. Georghiou (Greece) 192 pts

16. C. Stephen (G.B.) 191 pts
52. W. Campbell (Ireland) 175 pts
53. A. McMahon (Ireland) 174 pts

RAPID-FIRE PISTOL

1. J. Zapedzki (Poland) 595 pts
   (Olympic record)
2. L. Faita (Czechoslovakia) 594 pts
3. V. Torshin (U.S.S.R.) 593 pts
4. P. Buser (Switzerland) 592 pts
5. J. Gonzalez (Spain) 592 pts
6. G. Liverzani (Italy) 591 pts
7. F. Denev (Bulgaria) 590 pts
8. G. Petritsch (Austria) 590 pts

19. J. Cooke (G.B.) 585 pts
34. A. Clark (G.B.) 579 pts

SMALL-BORE RIFLE: PRONE

1. Ho Jun Li (North Korea) 599 pts
   (World record)
2. V. Auer (U.S.A.) 598 pts
3. N. Rotaru (Rumania) 598 pts
4. G. de Chirico (Italy) 597 pts
5. J. Vogler (Czechoslovakia) 597 pts
6. J. Santiago (Puerto Rico) 597 pts
7. L. Wigger (U.S.A.) 597 pts
8. L. Hammerl (Hungary) 597 pts

55. P. Lawrence (G.B.) 590 pts
    J. Palin (G.B.) 590 pts

CLAY PIGEON

1. A. Scalzone (Italy) 199 pts
   (World and Olympic record)
2. M. Carrega (France) 198 pts
3. S. Basagni (Italy) 195 pts
4. B. Hoppe (East Germany) 193 pts
5. J. Pahlsson (Sweden) 193 pts
6. J. Poindexter (U.S.A.) 192 pts
7. J. Primrose (Canada) 192 pts
8. M. Olsen (Brazil) 191 pts

21. R. Carter (G.B.) 186 pts
25. B. Bailey (G.B.) 185 pts

MOVING TARGET

1. L. Zhelemiak (U.S.S.R.) 569 pts
   (World and Olympic record)
2. H. Bellingrodt (Colombia) 565 pts
3. J. Kynoch (G.B.) 562 pts
4. V. Postoialov (U.S.S.R.) 560 pts
5. C. Zeisner (West Germany) 554 pts
6. G. Gaard (Sweden) 553 pts
7. G. Danne (West Germany) 551 pts
8. K.-A. Karlsson (Sweden) 551 pts

24. J. Anthony (G.B.) 527 pts

BASKETBALL

1. U.S.S.R.
2. U.S.A.
3. Cuba
4. Italy

FOOTBALL

1. Poland
2. Hungary
3. East Germany
4. U.S.S.R.

HANDBALL

1. Yugoslavia
2. Czechoslovakia
3. Rumania

HOCKEY

1. West Germany
2. Pakistan
3. India
4. Netherlands
5. Australia
6. Britain

VOLLEYBALL

MEN

1. Japan
2. East Germany
3. U.S.S.R.

WOMEN

1. U.S.S.R.
2. Japan
3. North Korea
4. South Korea

OLYMPIC MEDALS TABLE

	Gold	Silver	Bronze
U.S.S.R.	50	27	22
U.S.A.	33	31	30
East Germany	20	23	23
West Germany	13	11	16
Japan	13	8	8
Australia	8	7	2
Poland	7	5	9
Hungary	6	13	16
Bulgaria	6	10	5
Italy	5	3	10
Sweden	4	6	6
G.B.	4	5	9
Rumania	3	6	7
Finland	3	1	4
Cuba	3	1	4
Netherlands	3	1	1
France	2	4	7
Czechoslovakia	2	4	2
Kenya	2	3	4
Yugoslavia	2	1	2
Norway	2	1	1
North Korea	1	1	3
New Zealand	1	1	1
Uganda	1	1	0
Denmark	1	0	0
Switzerland	0	3	0
Canada	0	2	3
Iran	0	2	1
Belgium	0	2	0
Greece	0	2	0
Austria	0	1	2
Colombia	0	1	2
Mexico	0	1	0
Pakistan	0	1	0
Tunisia	0	1	0
Argentina	0	1	0
South Korea	0	1	0
Lebanon	0	1	0
Turkey	0	1	0
Mongolia	0	1	0
Brazil	0	0	2
Ethiopia	0	0	2
Spain	0	0	2
Jamaica	0	0	1
India	0	0	1
Niger	0	0	1
Ghana	0	0	1
Nigeria	0	0	1

Appendix
AVERY'S LAST STAND AT SAPPORO

Avery Brundage is a collector of oriental art, a millionaire and 84 years old. He has been called senile and stupid and is nicknamed 'Slavery Avery'. And yet I have a respect for him—a respect which would be much greater if I thought that he had a heart.

One Saturday at the end of January 1972 he flew into Sapporo, a city of one million inhabitants, the biggest city of the most northern of the Japanese islands, a city which has spent, over the past six years, one hundred million pounds on preparations for the 11th winter Olympic Games. He had with him, so it was said, a dossier containing forty-eight names of skiers who had allowed their names to be used for advertising purposes, thus offending against the Olympic code which Mr. Brundage, President of the International Olympic Committee, guards with a religious fervour. Several hundred manufacturers' agents, 1000 competitors and 3000 Press men awaited him, knowing that if he were to declare any of those skiers ineligible to take part, then a chain reaction would set in which could only lead to the disappearance of winter sports from the Olympic scene.

Two hours after landing he held a Press conference in the palatial Sapporo Park Hotel. He did not waste time on formalities. 'The Olympic Games,' he said, 'are a sports event and not a business enterprise. There have always been regulations prohibiting advertising in the Olympic facilities—the stadium and the village. This time we have added that there should be no advertising on the clothing or apparatus or on anything connected with the Games, and this prohibition will be strictly enforced. We think that a competitor who permits his name or photograph to be used to advertise any form of product becomes an agent of the manufacturer and denigrates the Games to a contest between manufacturers instead of a contest between sportsmen. This we cannot tolerate.'

Avery Brundage, in his last year as Chairman of the I.O.C., had thrown down his challenge. Before the week was out he was to win a hollow victory over an Austrian skier of peasant stock named Karl Schranz: and yet he will never win a true victory until he is able to change the ways of the world. Karl Schranz comes from what was once a small and poor village in the Austrian Alps. But then the world discovered the attractions of sliding down snow on a couple of wooden boards and a whole new recreational industry was born. Schranz, the son of an Alpine peasant, profited from this industry. He was good at sliding down snow and the men who made the boards thought it would be a good idea to employ him so that he used their boards to prove that they were the best in the world. So Karl Schranz prospered and he built himself a small hotel above the village —St. Anton—and he bought a car and he worked for Dr. Kneissl who is head of one of the biggest ski-manufacturers in the world. Schranz was a very good skier—he won three world championship gold medals and the regard of his fellow skiers who rated him as highly as Toni Sailer or Jean-Claude Killy, both of whom were triple Olympic gold medalists. And he was a nice man. Divina Galica, Britain's best downhill racer since the war, says: 'I love him'. And she does not mean it in a feminine way but as one athlete who loves another because of his honesty and courage—as every athlete loves Emil Zatopek. Karl Schranz had everything that he wanted, except for one thing—an Olympic gold medal. And Mr. Avery Brundage was determined that Mr. Schranz was not going to have an opportunity of winning that.

Quite rightly, Mr. Brundage has fulminated against commercialism ever since the 1968 winter Games in Grenoble, France, where he had to suffer the indignity of being driven around in a car with advertising slogans on it. But lately his statements have become more and more dramatic: skiing must put its house in order; skiing should not be in the Games; some skiers will find that we have evidence against them when they get to Sapporo. As he stepped off that plane in Sapporo and came to the Press conference there was no doubt that he was brandishing a gun—but was it loaded?

As soon as the questions started we knew that he had no bullets;

that he was going to name no names; and that he was going to have difficulty in proving what he knew to be true—that there were many skiers in the West who lived off their earnings as skiers.

But what neither Mr. Brundage nor we of the Press knew was that an interview was taking place in the recreation centre above the shops in the Olympic village between Karl Schranz and a knowledgeable American journalist by the name of Will Grimsley. Quietly Schranz thought aloud about Avery Brundage and Will Grimsley took it all down. His thoughts were not new—many top athletes had shared them for many years: 'If Mr. Brundage had been as poor as I was and as poor as many other athletes, I wonder if he wouldn't have had a different attitude,' thought Schranz. 'If we followed Mr. Brundage's recommendations to their true end, then the Olympics would be a competition only for the very rich.'

Neither Schranz nor Grimsley could have known how those mild words, printed the next day in the *Japan Times*, were to be waved about in the International Olympic Committee. Unwisely, Schranz had challenged Avery Brundage's authority and had given him a bullet to use in that gun. Forty-two members of the autocratic Olympic Committee were there in Sapporo and they debated the case of Karl Schranz. By 28 votes to 14 they voted that he be disqualified because of 'his activity and influence in the field of international alpine skiing competition and the manner in which he has permitted his name and his picture to be used in commercial advertising'. Many of those twenty-eight members who voted against Schranz did so because they felt they had to save the face of their old President, Avery Brundage, whom Schranz had openly challenged.

Before he was disqualified Schranz had threatened that if he was not allowed to compete he would tell all he knew. And the President of the Austrian Ski Federation, Dr. Klee, had said that if any one member of their team was disqualified then the whole of the Austrian Olympic team would return home in protest. So now the winter Games trembled on the brink of a disaster.

But the Austrians had too much to lose. They had built a special ski chalet in Sapporo, halfway between the Press Centre and the Olympic village, in which, every day, there were displays of the latest Austrian equipment and Austrian ski fashions. Over 10 per cent of the gross national product of Austria comes from ski equipment and from tourists who go to Austria to ski, so naturally none of these commercial interests wanted their team to withdraw. Neither did Schranz's team mates who were furious that he should have put their chances of competing in jeopardy. A compromise had to be found and of course a compromise was found. Schranz himself made a plea for the team to stay and carry on with the Games—and stay they did, much to the relief of their Japanese hosts. So one man was sacrificed in Brundage's crusade against professionalism—a crusade which would never get to the heart of the matter.

Let me illustrate that point with the story of the man who won the first gold medal of the Games—a small, powerful man, clothed in white, by the name of Vjaceslav Vedenin. He skied 30 kilometres (nearly 19 miles) in 1 hr 36 min 31·15 sec, beating two tall Norwegians, with ice on their eyebrows, by nearly a minute. His profession, according to the Swedes, is that of Skirunner. Surely there is no difference in status—amateur or professional—between this 29-year-old Russian and the 33-year-old Schranz. Vedenin lives in a Communist society. Now I cannot prove the circumstances of his life but it is impossible to imagine that he is, or will be, treated any differently from any other Honoured Master of Sport in Russia. He will have enough money, given by a grateful state, to buy a car, and he will go to the top of the long delivery queue that exists in all Communist states for such 'consumer durables' as motor cars. He will be well housed and when the time comes for him to need a job it will be a well paid job, congenial and secure. The state does all this for him, whereas in a capitalist society it is the athlete himself, Schranz, who has to make certain that he has a car, a secure home and a good job.

It is, if you like, no more than the difference between Communism and Capitalism and it only goes to prove how the whole amateur–professional argument is archaic and totally irrelevant to those people who take part in sport at its highest level. All the athletes want is the opportunity to compete against the best in the world. This view is shared, I believe, by every single athlete in the Olympic village whether he be an Englishman born to the ownership of acres of rich land, or a Norwegian wood-cutter.

But it is time we left the arguments behind and got on with the sport. Sapporo did its best to make certain that the sport would be good. They built the Alpine downhill courses on Mount Eniwa, a spectacular extinct volcano overhanging a beautiful lake. The whole area is a nature reserve but they invaded the reserve in the name of the Olympic Games and with the aid of six tons of explosives, 850 bulldozers and 15,000 men they built the downhill courses. It cost them one million pounds and at the end of the Games they were going to take it down again and restore the land to nature. Surely in a world in which thousands of people still die of hunger there is no more ridiculous example of conspicuous waste.

The first event on this course was the Women's Downhill, for which a buxom Austrian girl, Annemarie Proell, was the hot favourite. Her most serious rival was the French girl, Françoise Macchi, but unfortunately for Mademoiselle Macchi she had a complex about Annemarie. She thought that Annemarie had a better eye for the fastest line down the course and so whenever they went out training she trailed the big Austrian girl. Naturally this annoyed Annemarie so that, on one occasion, she slowed down so much that the French girl, following closely, had to take avoiding action and in doing so she fell and damaged her knee. Which just goes to prove that you do not win Olympic gold medals by following other people.

Neither was it Annemarie Proell who won. It was a pneumatic Swiss girl called Marie-Therese Nadig who started to ski when she was three. Annemarie Proell, who started to ski as soon as she could walk, came second and Susan Corrock of the United States who seems to have begun her skiing career a little late—when she was six—came third.

The four British girls came 23rd, 25th, 26th and 38th out of forty-four starters and that is not very good but hardly surprising because none of them were born on skis. What was surprising was that Divina Galica, the best British downhill racer, who should have been amongst the top fifteen, could only come 26th. It was also rather surprising that Annemarie Proell was beaten; and there is a connection between these two—a connection which started one hell of a row in Austria.

The connection is a little Austrian in his late thirties called Karl Kahr. He is one of the best ski trainers in the world and four years ago, when he was the trainer of the Austrian national team, the President of the Saltzburg Regional Ski Federation brought a 15-year-old schoolgirl to him. 'In ten years', he says in broken English, 'you see perhaps one talent like this. She is a very small girl and she falls down. But she always gets up. When I tell her that the course is too difficult for her, she cries, because I would not let her do it.' That girl was Miss Proell and she came from a farm—the last farm at the top of an Alpine valley—where she lived with her seven brothers and sisters. In summer she ran down the valley to school and in winter she skied down and then climbed back home—a climb which took an hour. She became a very strong girl. Three years later, under Mr. Kahr's tutelage, Miss Proell won the World Cup for skiing and Mr. Kahr was in trouble. He was, so the Austrian Ski Federation thought, devoting too much time to Miss Proell at the expense of other girls in the team. So he was sacked.

Mrs. Maria Goldberger, the astute Manager of the British women's team, saw the opportunity of getting a really world class trainer (generally the British have to choose from those left over after the big skiing nations have taken their pick), and so she hired Mr. Kahr. Thus he was in the Olympic village working for the British. But, of course, he was totally unable to say 'no' to his old protégée Annemarie Proell when she came to him for advice. Indeed, it crossed his mind that if she won the first gold medal of the Alpine events, and it could be shown that he had some part in it, then he might get his old job back. So it was that Mrs. Goldberger found Annemarie in the British team's waxing room, and it was obvious to her that Mr. Kahr had been waxing Annemarie's skis as he had waxed Divina Galica's. But waxing is a very difficult art. The day before the event Karl Kahr had told me that the race would be won by the person with the most appropriate wax: 'Every day it is snowing,' he said 'so the downhill is slow. The snow temperature is cold but the humidity is high, so it will be very difficult to wax.' And so it was and Mr. Kahr chose the wrong one.

I was sliding down the course outside the barriers as the best girls raced down. Miss Nadig, of Switzerland, in a crash hat that looked as if an artist's palette had fallen on it, and with start number 13, was working hard in that strange crouch position which the top skiers adopt—her thighs juddering to absorb the shocks and pressing down on the backs of her skis with all the weight of her rather large bottom as if trying to force her skis to go faster. Next came Divina Galica and even my untrained eye could see that she was going appreciably slower. Jeremy Palmer-Tomkinson (who was the double for Blofeld in the skiing sequences in the film 'On Her Majesty's Secret Service') was at the same spot and mouthing imprecations into the air: 'Can't the British ever get their wax right?' But it wasn't the British, it was Mr. Kahr.

Next came Annemarie Proell. She looked perfect to me, powerful and rhythmic, using what she calls her 'good nez' to pick the perfect line, but when the times filtered up through the trees from the loudspeakers at the finish, she was 0·32 seconds slower than Marie-Therese Nadig.

So Austria lost another potential gold medal because of the mistake of Karl Kahr and his blood will be demanded. It is difficult to find a parallel in British life. It is something more than the feeling there would have been if England had lost the World Cup final in 1966 because Sir Alf Ramsey put the team into the wrong boots. It is something more than that because skiing is so much a part of Austria's economy. So perhaps it would be truer to say that Mr. Kahr's crime is a cross between Sir Alf Ramsey putting the England team into the wrong boots and Lord Stokes deciding to make a car unfit for the market!

Two days later another Swiss skier won the Men's Downhill event: 23-year-old Bernhard Russi who streaked down approximately $1\frac{5}{8}$ miles of snow in 1 min 51·43 sec—an average of something over fifty-five miles an hour. His team mate, Collumbin, was second, just 0·64 seconds slower, and Heini Messner, the 32-year-old Austrian veteran, was 0·37 seconds slower to gain the bronze medal. With such small differences between first, second and third it is easy to appreciate how important the right wax is, how important the right skis are and how one mistake can cost you a medal. And such tiny margins are also vital to the vast equipment industries of the various nations. The skiing nations believe that once a Swiss skier, for instance, wins a gold medal everyone in the world will want to buy Swiss skis and learn to ski at a Swiss ski school or from a Swiss teacher, and they seem to be right. Take the case of Toni Sailer, the great Austrian skier who won three gold medals at the 1956 Olympics: five years later it was estimated that there were 200 Austrian ski instructors working in United States ski resorts compared with only four French instructors. But of course it is all a lot of nonsense.

No normal skier—indeed few really good skiers—could possibly handle the type of skis that these Olympic champions use. Besides who, when they're skiing for pleasure, is going to change his skis whenever he moves on to a different ski run. That is what these experts do. They have a different type of ski for different types of run and, of course, they have a vast entourage of ski manufacturers' agents, binding experts and waxing experts following in their wake. The plain fact is that the best skis for the ordinary recreational skier would be absolutely no good to an Olympic competitor—and vice-versa. But it does seem that there is something in human nature that makes the holiday skier prefer to buy the same make as that worn by the Olympic champion—just as any schoolboy wants a pair of Bobby Charlton football boots.

Four days after the opening ceremony 41 women and 55 men had completed the downhill course on Mount Eniwa. Not one of them had taken longer than three minutes and then we all went back to Sapporo and left the army of workmen to take down the stands, dismantle the timing equipment, break up the concrete which moored the ski-lifts to the mountain and return it all to nature. Has sport—and the Olympics—gone mad?

I escaped from the madness every morning to the cross-country course which was no more than a mile and a half from the Olympic village. There, in the stillness of a birch forest, one could put on a pair of very simple and very light skis and glide silently through the snow under one's own power. It seemed to me a sane and rational sport developed naturally from man's need to travel on his own feet across a snow-laden landscape. The men—and women—who won these cross-country events, the Nordic events as they are called, were genuine athletes who won because they were physically fitter and had paced themselves properly over fifteen or thirty or fifty kilometres. One could follow them round and get some good exercise and have time to appreciate the scenery and the skill and fitness of the competitors—an oasis of sanity in a strange and artificial world.

There's nothing more artificial than that mad sport known as Bobbing. It took an hour to drive northwards to Mount Teine where the Bob and Luge runs were situated. Halfway up the mountain one could look down on to the plains: to the right, towards the south-east, was a black pall of smoke underneath which lay the industrial city of Sapporo; to the left, towards the north-west, was the Sea of Japan across which, 400 miles away, lies Vladivostok and that limitless Siberian tundra that stretches to the Urals, the border between Europe and Asia. I can remember standing up there one day, the last but one day of the Winter Games, just after the four man Bob event had finished. Inside a long wooden shed the Bob teams of eleven nations were smearing thick axle grease on to the runners of their bobs and packing them away carefully for the long journey home. Outside, at the bottom of the Bob run, the successful team, the Swiss number 1 team, piloted by a 38-year-old garage owner, Jean Wicki, were receiving their medals from Mr. Avery Brundage who had just been created a member of the Order of the Rising Sun (first class) by the Emperor of Japan. The sun was shining and it was a lovely sparkling day, but six hours earlier another blizzard had come screeching in over the Sea of Japan from Siberia. This contrast in the weather symbolised the contrast of these Games.

There was only one common factor—the quality of the Japanese organisation. Nowhere did I hear one single complaint of any substance. They brought together one thousand athletes and three thousand Press and television men from all over the world and housed them on the outskirts of a new industrial city of one million people and they satisfied their every need with gentle courtesy and dignity. They did it by employing a massive number of highly disciplined people aided by every modern technological device. Their snow-removing plans for instance, were based on clearing a fall of one and a half feet of snow from 280 miles of roads in three hours —and when that amount of snow did fall overnight the plan worked. I could not imagine it happening in Sheffield and I am absolutely certain that I, and most of the people of Britain, would not want it to happen in our country. I have already mentioned the waste on Mount Eniwa and the same thing was due to happen on Mount Teine when the Bob run and the Luge run were scheduled to be removed. The cost of these facilities was nearly two million pounds and they will cost a few hundred thousand yen to knock down and restore the earth. And all this for ten days of highly artificial sport.

The competitors realised it as well. John Blewitt, one of the British speed skaters in Sapporo, said, rather bitterly: 'We are about the only true sport here. All we need is a patch of ice and a pair of skates and we own the skates ourselves.' But to me even his sport is a time trial. What I missed above all at these—and all the previous winter Games—is the sight of athlete against athlete. In the winter Olympics everything, except the ice hockey and the cross-country relay events, is a time trial. But then there are some people, some nations, who love time trials. Otherwise, why should Ard Schenk, who won three out of the four speed skating gold medals, be named as 'the man of the year', in Holland. Before the Games ended he flew home to capitalise on his fame—a fame which John Blewitt equates with that of George Best in Britain. He will make a lot of money but not too much, apparently, to have him barred from amateur competitions under the elastic amateur rules of speed skating.

Of course the problem for us British at these winter Games is that none of the sports are native to our own country. It is not like in Holland where speed skating grew up naturally as a way of travelling around their frozen canal system. Now they have developed it to the extent that there are seven specially constructed artificial ice tracks, each of four hundred metres, with another three on the drawing-board. I suppose that it is fun to watch when you understand it but we in Britain are not ever likely to understand it when there is not one single speed skating arena in the country. British speed skaters like John Blewitt have to make do with twice weekly sessions on Richmond ice rink—more suitable for hockey than for speed skating—and then those two sessions are at 6.30 on a Sunday morning for one and a half hours and between 10.15 and 11.30 on a Tuesday night. John Blewitt believes that if there was just one speed stadium in Britain and if some of our surplus distance runners could be persuaded to put on skates 'we'd be laughing'. And he points out that the stadium could be used in the summer by the roller skaters who up to now have trained on airfield runways. And trained so successfully that a man by the name of John Folley won a world championship in 1971. One picks up some odd information at these Olympics. And one has some odd feelings.

First and foremost of these is that the whole circus is getting out of all proportion. When Schranz went home to Austria he was welcomed by more people in Vienna than welcomed either President Kennedy or Queen Elizabeth. And while Austria was welcoming her martyr, France was in mourning because they had not won a single gold medal. Yet they had spent more time and money than any other nation on training and equipping their national team. I must confess that I felt myself in sympathy with the French member of Parliament who charged his government with spending too much on the national teams and not nearly enough on recreational sport for school children. He makes a good point which all sports and all nations should note. As the spotlight intensifies (and it has become pretty fierce when the proportion of Press and TV men to athletes has become 3 to 1) and as success apparently becomes more and more important for national pride and national economies, then the main purpose of sport—enjoyment and recreation—gets utterly lost.

SAPPORO 72—*RESULTS*

ALPINE SKIING

Men

DOWNHILL

Olympic Champion: J.-C. Killy (France)
World Champion: B. Russi (Switzerland)

1. B. Russi (Switzerland)	1 min 51·43 sec
2. R. Collumbin (Switzerland)	1 min 52·07 sec
3. H. Messner (Austria)	1 min 52·40 sec
4. A. Sprecher (Switzerland)	1 min 53·11 sec
5. E. Haaker (Norway)	1 min 53·16 sec
6. W. Tresch (Switzerland)	1 min 53·19 sec
7. K. Cordin (Austria)	1 min 53·32 sec
8. R. Cochran (U.S.A.)	1 min 53·39 sec
9. J. Loidl (Austria)	1 min 53·71 sec
10. M. Varallo (Italy)	1 min 53·85 sec
33. R. Varley (G.B.)	1 min 58·53 sec
37. A. Mapelli-Mozzi (G.B.)	2 min 00·28 sec
43 K. Bartelski (G.B.)	2 min 02·71 sec
50. I. Finlayson (G.B.)	2 min 06·50 sec

(55 started)

SLALOM

Olympic Champion: J.-C. Killy (France)
World Champion: J-N. Augert (France)

1. F. Ochoa (Spain)	1 min 49·27 sec
2. G. Thoeni (Italy)	1 min 50.28 sec
3. R. Thoeni (Italy)	1 min 50·30 sec
4. H. Duvillard (France)	1 min 50·45 sec
5. J-N. Augert (France)	1 min 50·51 sec
6. E. Schmalzl (Italy)	1 min 50·83 sec
7. D. Zwilling (Austria)	1 min 51·97 sec
8. E. Bruggmann (Switzerland)	1 min 52·03 sec
9. T. Palmer (U.S.A.)	1 min 52·05 sec
10. A. Bachleda-Curus (Poland)	1 min 52·26 sec
29. R. Varley (G.B.)	2 min 47·85 sec

GIANT SLALOM

Olympic Champion: J.-C. Killy (France)
World Champion: K. Schranz (Austria)

1. G. Thoeni (Italy)	3 min 09·62 sec
2. E. Bruggmann (Switzerland)	3 min 10·75 sec
3. W. Mattle (Switzerland)	3 min 10·99 sec
4. A. Hagn (West Germany)	3 min 11·16 sec
5. J-N. Augert (France)	3 min 11·84 sec
6. M. Rieger (West Germany)	3 min 11·94 sec
7. D. Zwilling (Austria)	3 min 12·32 sec
8. R. Tritscher (Austria)	3 min 12·39 sec
9. A. Bachleda (Poland)	3 min 12·42 sec
A. Penz (France)	3 min 12·42 sec

G.B. placings—I. Finlayson did not finish; K. Bartelski, R. Varley, A. Mapelli-Mozzi disqualified. (59 started)

ALPINE SKIING

Women

DOWNHILL

Olympic Champion: O. Pall (Austria)
World Champion: A. Zryd (Sweden)

1.	M-T. Nadig (Switzerland)	1 min 36·68 sec
2.	A-M. Proell (Austria)	1 min 37·00 sec
3.	S. Corrock (U.S.A.)	1 min 37·68 sec
4.	I. Mir (France)	1 min 38·62 sec
5.	R. Speiser (West Germany)	1 min 39·10 sec
6.	R. Mittermaier (West Germany)	1 min 39·32 sec
7.	B. Zurbriggen (Switzerland)	1 min 39·49 sec
8.	A. Famose (France)	1 min 39·70 sec
9.	B. Rauter (Austria)	1 min 39·84 sec
10.	M. Buehler (Liechtenstein)	1 min 40·06 sec
23.	V. Iliffe (G.B.)	1 min 41·36 sec
25.	G. Hathorn (G.B.)	1 min 41·42 sec
26.	D. Galica (G.B.)	1 min 41·58 sec
38.	C. Blackwood (G.B.)	1 min 44·61 sec

(41 started)

SLALOM

Olympic Champion: M. Goitschel (France)
World Champion: I. Lafforgue (France)

1.	B. Cochran (U.S.A.)	91·24 sec
2.	D. Debernard (France)	91·26 sec
3.	F. Steurer (France)	92·69 sec
4.	J. Crawford (Canada)	93·95 sec
5.	A-M. Proell (Austria)	94·03 sec
6.	P. Behr (West Germany)	94·27 sec
7.	Y. Kaserer (Austria)	94·36 sec
8.	P. Boydstun (U.S.A.)	95·59 sec
9.	S. Corrock (U.S.A.)	95·76 sec
	T. Foerland (Norway)	95·76 sec
11.	G. Hathorn (G.B.)	96·18 sec
15.	D. Galica (G.B.)	100·50 sec

(41 started)

GIANT SLALOM

Olympic Champion: N. Greene (Canada)
World Champion: B. Clifford (Canada)

1.	M-T. Nadig (Switzerland)	1 min 29·09 sec
2.	A-M. Proell (Austria)	1 min 30·75 sec
3.	W. Drexel (Austria)	1 min 32·35 sec
4.	L. Kreiner (Canada)	1 min 32·48 sec
5.	R. Speiser (West Germany)	1 min 32·56 sec
6.	F. Steurer (France)	1 min 32·59 sec
7.	D. Galica (G.B.)	1 min 32·72 sec
8.	B. Lafforgue (France)	1 min 32·08 sec
9.	T. Treichl (West Germany)	1 min 33·08 sec
10.	M. Buehler (Liechtenstein)	1 min 33·15 sec
14.	G. Hathorn (G.B.)	1 min 33·57 sec
26.	V. Iliffe (G.B.)	1 min 36·68 sec

(42 started)

NORDIC SKIING

Men

15 KILOMETRES

Olympic Champion: H. Groenningen (Norway)
World Champion: L-G. Asland (Sweden)

1.	S-A. Lundback (Sweden)	45 min 28·24 sec
2.	F. Simaschov (U.S.S.R.)	46 min 00·84 sec
3.	I. Formo (Norway)	46 min 02·68 sec
4.	J. Mieto (Finland)	46 min 02·74 sec
5.	Y. Skovobov (U.S.S.R.)	46 min 04·59 sec
6.	A. Lesser (East Germany)	46 min 17·01 sec
7.	W. Demel (West Germany)	46 min 17·36 sec
8.	G. Larsson (Sweden)	46 min 23·29 sec
9.	O. Braa (Norway)	46 min 25·11 sec
10.	O. Karjalainen (Finland)	46 min 27·51 sec
59.	T. Palliser (G.B.)	54 min 11·98 sec
60.	P. Strong (G.B.)	54 min 41·99 sec
61.	H. Tobin (G.B.)	56 min 05·05 sec

(62 started)

30 KILOMETRES

Olympic Champion: F. Nones (Italy)
World Champion: V. Vedenin (U.S.S.R.)

1.	V. Vedenin (U.S.S.R.)	1 hr 36 min 33·15 sec
2.	P. Tyldum (Norway)	1 hr 37 min 25·30 sec
3.	J. Harviken (Norway)	1 hr 37 min 32·44 sec
4.	G. Larsson (Sweden)	1 hr 37 min 33·72 sec
5.	W. Demel (West Germany)	1 hr 37 min 45·5 sec
6.	F. Simaschov (U.S.S.R.)	1 hr 38 min 22·5 sec
7.	A. Kalin (Switzerland)	1 hr 38 min 40·72 sec
8.	G. Klause (East Germany)	1 hr 39 min 15·54 sec
9.	S. Henych (Czechoslovakia)	1 hr 39 min 24·29 sec
10.	G. Gehring (East Germany)	1 hr 39 min 44·47 sec
54.	K. Oliver (G.B.)	1 hr 54 min 10·6 sec
55.	T. Palliser (G.B.)	1 hr 54 min 39·41 sec

(59 started)

50 KILOMETRES

Olympic Champion: O. Ellefsaeter (Norway)
World Champion: K. Oikarainen (Finland)

1. P. Tyldum (Norway) 2 hr 43 min 14·75 sec
2. M. Myrmo (Norway) 2 hr 43 min 29·45 sec
3. V. Vedenin (U.S.S.R.) 2 hr 44 min 00·19 sec
4. R. Hjermstad (Norway) 2 hr 44 min 14·61 sec
5. W. Demel (West Germany) 2 hr 44 min 32·57 sec
6. W. Geeser (Switzerland) 2 hr 44 min 34·13 sec
7. L. Bollig (Sweden) 2 hr 45 min 06·8 sec
8. F. Simaschov (U.S.S.R.) 2 hr 45 min 08·93 sec
9. G. Klause (East Germany) 2 hr 46 min 17·43 sec
10. O. Ellefsaeter (Norway) 2 hr 46 min 46·94 sec

(40 started)

COMBINED

Olympic Champion: F. Keller (West Germany)
World Champion: L. Rygl (Czechoslovakia)

1.	U. Wehling (East Germany)	413·34 pts
2.	R. Miettinen (Finland)	405·50 pts
3.	K. Luck (East Germany)	398·80 pts
4.	E. Kilpinen (Finland)	391·84 pts
5.	Y. Katsuro (Japan)	390·20 pts
6.	T. Kucra (Czechoslovakia)	387·93 pts
7.	A. Nossov (U.S.S.R.)	387·73 pts
8.	K. Berg (Norway)	384·80 pts
9.	G. Deckers (East Germany)	382·97 pts
10.	R. Pohland (West Germany)	381·19 pts

(39 started)

RELAY

Olympic Champions: Norway
World Champions: U.S.S.R.

1.	U.S.S.R.	2 hr 4 min 47 sec
2.	Norway	2 hr 4 min 57 sec
3.	Switzerland	2 hr 7 min 00 sec
4.	Sweden	2 hr 7 min 3 sec
5.	Finland	2 hr 7 min 50 sec
6.	East Germany	2 hr 10 min 3 sec
7.	West Germany	2 hr 10 min 42 sec
8.	Czechoslovakia	2 hr 11 min 27 sec
9.	Italy	2 hr 12 min 7 sec
10.	Japan	2 hr 13 min 59 sec

70 METRES JUMP

Olympic Champion: J. Raska (Czechoslovakia)
World Champion: G. Napalkov (U.S.S.R.)

1.	V. Kasaya (Japan)	244·2 pts
2.	A. Konno (Japan)	234·8 pts
3.	S. Aochi (Japan)	229·5 pts
4.	I. Mork (Norway)	225·5 pts
5.	J. Raska (Czechoslovakia)	224·8 pts
6.	W. Fortuna (Poland)	222·0 pts
7.	G. Napalkov (U.S.S.R.)	220·2 pts
	K. Kodejska (Czechoslovakia)	220·2 pts
9.	K. Tsakadze (U.S.S.R.)	219·9 pts
10.	P. Stefancic (Yugoslavia)	218·1 pts

(56 started)

90 METRES JUMP

Olympic Champion: V. Belousov (U.S.S.R)
World Champion: G. Napalkov (U.S.S.R.)

1.	W. Fortuna (Poland)	219·9 pts
2.	W. Steiner (Switzerland)	219·8 pts
3.	R. Schmidt (East Germany)	219·3 pts
4.	T. Kaeyhkoe (Finland)	219·2 pts
5.	M. Wolf (East Germany)	215·1 pts
6.	G. Napalkov (U.S.S.R.)	210·1 pts
7.	Y. Kasaya (Japan)	209·4 pts
8.	D. Pudgar (Yugoslavia)	206·0 pts
9.	E. Rautionaho (Finland)	205·8 pts
10.	J. Raska (Czechoslovakia)	204·7 pts

(52 started)

NORDIC SKIING

Women

5 KILOMETRES

Olympic Champion: T. Gustafsson (Sweden)
World Champion: G. Koulacova (U.S.S.R.)

1.	G. Koulacova (U.S.S.R.)	17 min 00·5 sec
2.	M. Kajosmaa (Finland)	17 min 0·55 sec
3.	H. Sikolova (Czechoslovakia)	17 min 07·32 sec
4.	A. Olyunina (U.S.S.R.)	17 min 07·41 sec
5.	H. Kuntola (Finland)	17 min 11·67 sec
6.	L. Moukhatcheva (U.S.S.R.)	17 min 12·08 sec
7.	B. Morrdre Lammedal (Norway)	17 min 16·79 sec
8.	A. Dahl (Norway)	17 min 17·49 sec
9.	H. Takalo (Finland)	17 min 21·39 sec
10.	N. Fedorova (U.S.S.R.)	17 min 25·62 sec
42.	F. Lutken (G.B.)	19 min 40·17 sec

(43 started)

10 KILOMETRES

Olympic Champion: G. Gustafsson (Sweden)
World Champion: A. Oluynina (U.S.S.R.)

1.	G. Koulacova (U.S.S.R.)	34 min 17·80 sec
2.	A. Olyunina (U.S.S.R.)	34 min 54·11 sec
3.	M. Kajosmaa (Finland)	34 min 56·45 sec
4.	L. Moukhatcheva (U.S.S.R.)	34 min 58·56 sec
5.	H. Takalo (Finland)	35 min 06·34 sec
6.	A. Dahl (Norway)	35 min 18·84 sec
7.	H. Sikolova (Czechoslovakia)	35 min 29·33 sec
8.	H. Kuntola (Finland)	35 min 36·71 sec
9.	R. Fisher (East Germany)	35 min 46·96 sec
10.	N. Chebalina (U.S.S.R.)	35 min 54·59 sec
39.	F. Lutken (G.B.)	40 min 02·73 sec

(21 started)

RELAY

1.	Soviet Union	48 min 46·15 sec
2.	Finland	49 min 19·37 sec
3.	Norway	49 min 51·49 sec
4.	West Germany	50 min 25·61 sec
5.	East Germany	50 min 28·45 sec
6.	Czechoslovakia	51 min 16·16 sec
7.	Poland	51 min 49·13 sec
8.	Sweden	51 min 51·84 sec
9.	Japan	53 min 20·75 sec
10.	Canada	53 min 37·82 sec

BIATHLON

INDIVIDUAL

Olympic Champion: M. Solberg (Norway)
World Champion: D. Speer (East Germany)

1.	M. Solberg (Norway)	1 hr 15 min 55·5 sec
2.	H. Knauthe (East Germany)	1 hr 16 min 07·6 sec
3.	L. Arwidson (Sweden)	1 hr 16 min 27·0 sec
4.	A. Tikhonov (U.S.S.R.)	1 hr 16 min 48·6 sec
5.	Y. Salpakari (Finland)	1 hr 16 min 51·2 sec
6.	E. Saira (Finland)	1 hr 17 min 34·8 sec
7.	V. Mamatov (U.S.S.R.)	1 hr 18 min 16·26 sec
8.	T. Svendsberget (Norway)	1 hr 18 min 26·54 sec
9.	A. Klima (Poland)	1 hr 19 min 00·86 sec
10.	D. Caludon (France)	1 hr 19 min 14·67 sec
11.	K. Oliver (G.B.)	1 hr 20 min 40·31 sec
26.	J. Stevens (G.B.)	1 hr 23 min 28·95 sec
43.	A. Notley (G.B.)	1 hr 28 min 48·72 sec
53.	M. Hirst (G.B.)	1 hr 34 min 55·59 sec

(53 started)

RELAY

Olympic Champions: U.S.S.R.
World Champions: U.S.S.R.

1.	U.S.S.R.	1 hr 51 min 34·92 sec
2.	Finland	1 hr 54 min 37·25 sec
3.	East Germany	1 hr 54 min 57·67 sec
4.	Norway	1 hr 56 min 24·41 sec
5.	Sweden	1 hr 56 min 57·40 sec
6.	U.S.A.	1 hr 57 min 24·32 sec
7.	Poland	1 hr 58 min 09·92 sec
8.	Japan	1 hr 59 min 09·48 sec
9.	Rumania	1 hr 59 min 30·61 sec
10.	Italy	1 hr 59 min 47·62 sec
11.	G.B.	2 hr 01 min 38·84 sec

(13 started)

BOBSLEIGH

TWO-MAN

Olympic Champions: Italy
World Champions: Italy

1.	W. Zimmerer and P. Utzschneider (West Germany 2)	4 min 57·07 sec
2.	H. Floth and P. Bader (West Germany 1)	4 min 58·84 sec
3.	J. Wicki and E. Hubacher (Switzerland 1)	4 min 59·33 sec
4.	G. Gaspari and M. Armano (Italy 1)	5 min 00·45 sec
5.	I. Panturu and I. Zangor (Rumania 1)	5 min 00·53 sec
6.	C. Eriksson and J. Johansson (Sweden 1)	5 min 01·40 sec
7.	H. Candrian and H. Schenker (Switzerland 2)	5 min 01·44 sec
8.	H. Gruber and J. Oberhauser (Austria 1)	5 min 01·60 sec
9.	P. Parisot and A. Roy (France 1)	5 min 03·46 sec
10.	E. Vicarlo and C. Del Fabbro (Italy 2)	5 min 03·66 sec
17.	J. Hammond and M. Sweet (G.B.)	5 min 06·96 sec
18.	P. Evelyn and P. Clifford (G.B.)	

(21 started)

FOUR-MAN

Olympic Champions: Italy
World Champions: Italy

1.	Switzerland 1 (Wicki, Hubacher, Leutenegger, Carmichel)	4 min 43·07 sec
2.	Italy 1	4 min 42·83 sec
3.	West Germany 1	4 min 42·92 sec
4.	Switzerland 2	4 min 44·56 sec
5.	West Germany 2	4 min 45·09 sec
6.	Austria 1	4 min 45·77 sec
7.	Austria 2	4 min 46·66 sec
8.	Italy 2	4 min 46·73 sec
9.	France 1	4 min 46·75 sec
10.	Rumania 1	4 min 47·12 sec
15.	G.B. 2	4 min 50·46 sec
16.	G.B. 1	4 min 51·03 sec

LUGE

INDIVIDUAL MEN

Olympic Champion: M. Schmid (Austria)
World Champion: K. Brunner (Italy)

1.	W. Scheidel (East Germany)	3 min 27·58 sec
2.	H. Ehrig (East Germany)	3 min 28·39 sec
3.	W. Fiedler (East Germany)	3 min 28·73 sec
4.	K. Bonsack (East Germany)	3 min 29·16 sec
5.	L. Nagenrauft (West Germany)	3 min 29·67 sec
6.	J. Fendt (West Germany)	3 min 30·03 sec
7.	M. Schmid (Austria)	3 min 30·05 sec
8.	P. Hildgartner (Italy)	3 min 30·55 sec
9.	K. Brunner (Italy)	3 min 30·87 sec
10.	J. Feistmantl (Austria)	3 min 31·32 sec
34.	J. Woodall (G.B.)	3 min 40·15 sec
40.	J. Palmer-Tomkinson (G.B.)	3 min 43·61 sec
42.	R. Liversedge (G.B.)	3 min 46·49 sec
43.	R. Deen (G.B.)	3 min 55·54 sec

(44 started)

INDIVIDUAL WOMEN

Olympic Champion: E. Lechner (Italy)
World Champion: E. Demleitner (West Germany)

1.	A. Muller (East Germany)	2 min 59·18 sec
2.	U. Ruehrold (East Germany)	2 min 59·49 sec
3.	M. Schumann (East Germany)	2 min 59·54 sec
4.	E. Demleitner (West Germany)	3 min 00·80 sec
5.	Y. Otaka (Japan)	3 min 00·98 sec
6.	W. Martyka (Poland)	3 min 02·33 sec
	H. Kanasz (Poland)	3 min 02·33 sec
8.	S. Felder (Italy)	3 min 02·90 sec
9.	B. Piecha (Poland)	3 min 03·07 sec
10.	C. Schmuck (West Germany)	3 min 03·19 sec

(22 started)

TWO-MAN

Olympic Champions: E. Bonsack and T. Koehler (East Germany)

World Champions: P. Hildgartner and W. Plaikner (Italy)

1. P. Hildgartner and W. Plaikner (Italy) 1 min 28·35 sec
H. Hornlein and R. Bredow (East Germany) 1 min 28·35 sec
3. K. Bonsack and W. Fielder (East Germany) 1 min 29·16 sec
4. S. Aral and M. Kobayashi (Japan) 1 min 29·63 sec
5. H. Brandner and B. Schwarm (West Germany) 1 min 29·66 sec
M. Wieckowski and W. Kubik (Poland) 1 min 29·66 sec
7. M. Schmid and E. Walch (Austria) 1 min 29·75 sec
8. S. Mair and E. Mair (Italy) 1 min 30·26 sec
9. R. Schmid and F. Schachner (Austria) 1 min 30·68 sec
L. Kudzia and R. Gawlor (Poland) 1 min 30·68 sec
19. J. Woodall and S. March (G.B.) 1 min 33·92 sec
20. J. Palmer-Tomkinson and M. de Carvalho (G.B.) 1 min 34·59 sec

(20 started)

FIGURE-SKATING

MEN

Olympic Champion: W. Shwarz (Austria)

World Champion: O. Nepela (Czechoslovakia)

(Placement/points)

1. O. Nepela (Czechoslovakia) 9/2739·1
2. S. Tchetveroukhin (U.S.S.R.) 20/2672·4
3. P. Pera (France) 28/2653·1
4. K. Shelley (U.S.A.) 43/2596·0
5. J. Petkevich (U.S.A.) 47/2591·5
6. J. Hoffmann (East Germany) 55/2567·6
7. H. Oundjian (G.B.) 65/2538·8
8. V. Kovalev (U.S.S.R.) 80/2521·6
9. T. Cranston (Canada) 80·5/2517·2
10. G. McKellen (U.S.A.) 89/2511·0
11. J. Curry (G.B.) 95/2512·2

(17 started)

WOMEN

Olympic Champion: P. Fleming (U.S.A.)

World Champion: B. Schuba (Austria)

(Placements/points)

1. B. Schuba (Austria) 9/2751·5
2. K. Magnusson (Canada) 23/2673·2
3. J. Lynn (U.S.A.) 27/2663·1
4. J. Holmes (U.S.A.) 39/2627·0
5. Z. Almassy (Hungary) 47/2592·4
6. S. Morgenstern (East Germany) 53/2579·4
7. R. Trapanese (Italy) 55/254·8
8. C. Errath (East Germany) 78/2489·3
9. C. Walter (Switzerland) 86/2467·3
10. K. Yamashita (Japan) 93/2449·9
11. J. Scott (G.B.) 101/2436·8

(19 started)

PAIRS

Olympic Champions: O. Protopopov and L. Belusova (U.S.S.R.)

World Champions: I. Rodnina and A. Ulanov (U.S.S.R.)

(Placements/points)

1. I. Rodnina and A. Ulanov (U.S.S.R.) 12/420·4
2. L. Smirnova and A. Sourakin (U.S.S.R.) 15/419·4
3. M. Cross and U. Kagelmann (East Germany) 29/411·8
4. J. Starbuck and K. Shelley (U.S.A.) 35/406·8
5. A. Lehmann and H. Weisinger (West Germany) 52/399·8
6. I. Tcherniaeva and V. Blagov (U.S.S.R.) 52/399·1
7. M. & M. Militano (U.S.A.) 65·5/393·0
8. A. Kansy and A. Salzmann (East Germany) 84/384·9
9. S. and V. Bezic (Canada) 84/384·9
10. C. Halke and E. Rausch (West Germany) 87/381·1
14. L. Connolly and C. Taylforth (G.B.) 126/360·6

(16 started)

SPEED-SKATING

Men

500 METRES

Olympic Champion: E. Keller (West Germany)
World Champion: D. Fornaes (Norway)

1. E. Keller (West Germany)	39·44 sec
2. H. Borjes (Sweden)	39·69 sec
3. V. Mouratov (U.S.S.R.)	39·80 sec
4. P. Bjorang (Norway)	39·91 sec
5. S. Hanninen (Finland)	40·12 sec
6. L. Linkovesi (Finland)	40·14 sec
7. O. Konig (Sweden)	40·25 sec
8. M. Suzuki (Japan)	40·35 sec
9. M. Wallberg (Sweden)	40·41 sec
10. H. Lichtenstern (West Germany)	40·55 sec
24. D. Hampton (G.B.)	42·59 sec

(36 started)

1500 METRES

Olympic Champion: C. Verkerk (Netherlands)
World Champion: A. Schenk (Netherlands)

1. A. Schenk (Netherlands)	2 min 02·96 sec
2. R. Gronvold (Norway)	2 min 04·26 sec
3. G. Claesson (Sweden)	2 min 05·89 sec
4. B. Tveter (Norway)	2 min 05·94 sec
5. J. Bols (Netherlands)	2 min 06·58 sec
6. V. Lavrouchkin (U.S.S.R.)	2 min 07·16 sec
7. D. Carroll (U.S.A.)	2 min 07·24 sec
8. C. Verkerk (Netherlands)	2 min 07·43 sec
9. J. Hoeglin (Sweden)	2 min 08·11 sec
10. K. Koskinen (Finland)	2 min 08·18 sec
37. J. Blewitt (G.B.)	2 min 18·96 sec

(39 started)

5000 METRES

Olympic Champion: F. Maier (Netherlands)
World Champion: A. Schenk (Netherlands)

1. A. Schenk (Netherlands)	7 min 23·61 sec
2. R. Gronvold (Norway)	7 min 28·18 sec
3. S. Stensen (Norway)	7 min 33·39 sec
4. G. Claesson (Sweden)	7 min 36·17 sec
5. W. Olsen (Norway)	7 min 36·47 sec
6. K. Verkerk (Netherlands)	7 min 39·17 sec
7. V. Lavrouchkin (U.S.S.R.)	7 min 39·26 sec
8. J. Bols (Netherlands)	7 min 39·40 sec
9. G. Zimmerman (West Germany)	7 min 41·16 sec
10. D. Carroll (U.S.A.)	7 min 44·72 sec
22. D. Hampton (G.B.)	8 min 07·85 sec
26. J. Blewitt (G.B.)	8 min 16·75 sec

(28 started)

10,000 METRES

Olympic Champion: J. Hoeglin (Sweden)
World Champion: A. Schenk (Netherlands)

1. A. Schenk (Netherlands)	15 min 01·35 sec
2. C. Verkerk (Netherlands)	15 min 04·70 sec
3. S. Stensen (Norway)	15 min 07·08 sec
4. J. Bols (Netherlands)	15 min 17·99 sec
5. V. Lavrouchkin (U.S.S.R.)	15 min 20·08 sec
6. T. Claesson (Sweden)	15 min 30·19 sec
7. K. Koskinen (Finland)	15 min 38·87 sec
8. G. Zimmermann (West Germany)	15 min 43·92 sec
9. D. Carroll (U.S.A.)	15 min 44·41 sec
10. K. Ito (Japan)	14 min 48·17 sec
20. D. Hampton (G.B.)	16 min 39·01 sec
23. J. Blewitt (G.B.)	16 min 51·50 sec

(42 started)

SPEED-SKATING

Women

500 METRES

Olympic Champion: L. Titova (U.S.S.R.)
World Champion: A. Henning (U.S.A.)

1. A. Henning (U.S.A.)	43·30 sec
2. V. Krasnova (U.S.S.R.)	44·01 sec
3. L. Titova (U.S.S.R.)	44·45 sec
4. S. Young (U.S.A.)	44·53 sec
5. M. Pflug (West Germany)	33·75 sec
6. A. Keulen-Deelstra (Netherlands)	44·89 sec
7. K. Lunda (U.S.A.)	44·95 sec
8. A. Boutova (U.S.S.R.)	45·17 sec
9. S. Saito (Japan)	45·36 sec
10. E. van de Brom (Netherlands)	45·62 sec

(28 started)

1000 METRES

Olympic Champion: C. Geijssen (Netherlands)
World Champion: D. Holum (U.S.A.)

1. M. Pflug (West Germany)	1 min 31·40 sec
2. A. Keulen-Deelstra (Netherlands)	1 min 31·61 sec
3. A. Henning (U.S.A.)	1 min 31·62 sec
4. L. Titova (U.S.S.R.)	1 min 31·85 sec
5. N. Statkevitch (U.S.S.R.)	1 min 32·21 sec
6. D. Holum (U.S.A.)	1 min 32·41 sec
7. E. van de Brom (Netherlands)	1 min 32·60 sec
8. S. Burka (Canada)	1 min 32·95 sec
9. S. Sundby (Norway)	1 min 33·05 sec
10. L. Savroulina (U.S.S.R.)	1 min 33·41 sec

(33 started)

1500 METRES

Olympic Champion: K. Mustonen (Finland)
World Champion: N. Statkevich (U.S.S.R.)

1.	D. Holum (U.S.A.)	2 min 20·85 sec
2.	S. Baas-Kaiser (Netherlands)	2 min 21·05 sec
3.	A. Keulen-Deelstra (Netherlands)	2 min 22.05 sec
4.	E. Van den Brom (Netherlands)	2 min 22·27 sec
5.	R. Taupadel (East Germany)	2 min 22·35 sec
6.	N. Statkevitch (U.S.S.R.)	2 min 23·19 sec
7.	C. Carpenter (U.S.A.)	2 min 23·93 sec
8.	S. Sundby (Norway)	2 min 24·07 sec
9.	K. Seregvina (U.S.S.R.)	2 min 24·29 sec
10.	M. Pflug (West Germany)	2 min 24·69 sec

(31 started)

3000 METRES

Olympic Champion: J. Schut (Netherlands)
World Champion: S. Kaiser (Netherlands)

1.	S. Kaiser (Netherlands)	4 min 52·14 sec
2.	D. Holum (U.S.A.)	4 min 58·67 sec
3.	A. Keulen-Deelstra (Netherlands)	4 min 59·91 sec
4.	S. Tigchelaar (Netherlands)	5 min 01·67 sec
5.	N. Statchelaar (U.S.S.R.)	5 min 01·79 sec
6.	K. Sereguina (U.S.S.R.)	5 min 01·88 sec
7.	T. Vilkas (Finland)	5 min 05·92 sec
8.	L. Savroulina (U.S.S.R.)	5 min 06·61 sec
9.	G. Ghan (North Korea)	5 min 07·24 sec
10.	S. Sundby (Norway)	5 min 07·76 sec

ICE HOCKEY FINAL TABLE

	P	W	D	L	F	A	Pts
U.S.S.R.	5	4	1	0	33	13	9
U.S.A.	5	3	0	2	18	15	6
Czechoslovakia	5	3	0	2	26	13	6
Sweden	5	2	1	2	17	13	5
Finland	5	2	0	3	14	24	4
Poland	5	0	0	5	9	39	0

SAPPORO MEDALS TABLE

	Gold	Silver	Bronze	Total
U.S.S.R.	8	5	3	16
East Germany	4	3	7	14
Switzerland	4	3	3	10
Holland	4	3	2	9
United States	3	2	3	8
West Germany	3	1	1	5
Norway	2	5	5	12
Italy	2	2	1	5
Austria	1	2	2	5
Sweden	1	1	2	4
Japan	1	1	1	3
Czechoslovakia	1	0	2	3
Poland	1	0	0	1
Spain	1	0	0	1
Finland	0	4	1	5
France	0	1	2	3
Canada	0	1	0	1

Two gold medals were awarded for a dead-heat in the two-man luge.